This book

CHILDREN AT RISK

Children
at Risk

DAVID PORTER

KINGSWAY PUBLICATIONS

EASTBOURNE

ISBN 0 86065 374 9

Biblical quotations are from the New International Version,
© New York International Bible Society 1978.

Front cover photo: Barbara Kreye, The Image Bank

Printed in Great Britain for
KINGSWAY PUBLICATIONS LTD
Lottbridge Drove, Eastbourne, E. Sussex BN23 6NT by
Richard Clay (The Chaucer Press) Ltd, Bungay, Suffolk.
Typeset by CST, Eastbourne, E. Sussex.

To
three campaigners:
Frederic Wertham, Mary Whitehouse
and Charles Oxley

Contents

Foreword

Children are not just tomorrow's adults—they are young citizens of today's society. They live in the age of computers and videos, drugs on the street and at the school gate. We are all vulnerable to those particular dangers that the eighties have brought along, but children are especially at risk, because they are still forming impressions of the world. What they take in, and the rate at which they learn, is crucial to their development as persons made in the image of God. We need to show them the long-term benefits of avoiding the cheap heroics readily provided by those who will not be around to pick up the broken pieces.

I have children, and chances are if you're reading this then you do too. Maybe you're a teacher, or you care for them in some other way. I hope you'll find David Porter's book helpful—not just to tell you about some of the challenges that face our youngsters today, though that's important. I hope that you'll be encouraged to go on caring, to go on working for the benefit and protection of our children. We owe it to ourselves, and we owe it to them and their children.

ROY CASTLE

Preface

I have had a very great deal of help in writing this book. Parents, teachers and counsellors have discussed the issues with me and enlarged my own thinking; organizations have answered my questions over the telephone and sent me detailed information by post; several firms have given me review copies of books and games; and some very busy people have given me generous amounts of their time.

In several of the areas covered in this book, events were moving rapidly forward as the manuscript went to press. In particular, government action on drug smuggling and drug peddling was, in early 1986, gathering considerable momentum. The concern which such developments illustrate reinforces the impression that I gained while researching the book: that not since Shaftesbury have so many children been at risk in our society, and that not since Shaftesbury have so many people been active in bringing about social change to protect them.

Some of the material in this book has already appeared in a booklet issued by the Evangelical Alliance in August 1985.

I would like to acknowledge particularly the help of the following, and to apologize for any inadvertent omissions: Bedford Square Press*, Beyond Software*, Dave Brown, Clive Calver, CARE Trust, Charles Cartwright, the Cope family, Ian Cooper, Deo Gloria Trust, Tim Dean, Heather

Dolman, Ros Draper, Eleanor, Peter Elsom, Edward England, Evangelical Alliance, Games Workshop Ltd*, Prabhu Guptara, Mark Harvey, Richard Herkes, Hewson Consultants*, John Lewis Partnership *Gazette*, Kingsway Publications*, Lauren, Edward Law, Lion Publishing*, West Liss Software Library, National Council for Voluntary Organisations, National Society for the Prevention of Cruelty to Children, Order of Christian Unity, Charles Oxley, Hamish Robertson, Scripture Union*, 10 Downing Street Press Office, Mary Whitehouse, Virgin Games Centre, Richard Winter.
* = supplied review copies.

And, most of all, to my wife Tricia.

DAVID PORTER
Greatham, 1985

I

Children at Risk

Children are at risk today. No day goes by without the newspapers or the television and radio announcing the latest statistics for child-related crime or giving an account of an incident in which a child has suffered through the cruelty or irresponsibility of adults.

In this book we will be looking at a number of those areas in which young children are, in one way or another, at risk. By 'young' I mean fourteen years old and younger. Most of the issues we will be discussing are problems that have either developed comparatively recently, or which have recently been the subject of a great deal of attention in the media.

I write as a Christian parent—I have two daughters, one two years old, the other eight. I also have a number of nieces and nephews in this age group. As I have watched these children grow I have often been alarmed and saddened by some of the choices that they are forced to make, even at an early age, by the society in which they live.

This book is intended to help parents, teachers, and anybody else concerned with young children, to give support and help to the children with whom they are involved.

There are three things that it sets out to do.

Firstly, it is *a handbook of information*. It contains information, and facts and figures, which I hope will prove illuminating and helpful. I have also talked to a great many of the people—some Christians, some not—who are working in the areas I deal with, as counsellors, manufacturers, distributors, commentators, etc. Their comments have been incorporated where appropriate.

So I hope that the chapters that follow will be a useful reference source for facts and background. Also, I want to alert adults to some disturbing developments which they may not have looked at closely, which they may not have known about, or which they may have thought were not a direct problem in their part of the country or their domestic situation.

Secondly, it sets out to be *a guidebook for concerned parents*. Having identified areas where our children are at risk, we go on to consider how we can best help our children to cope with the influences that surround them. The book contains information on recognizing danger signs, organizations that can help, and suggestions on how you yourself can best help your children.

We also consider ways to help children who have become seriously involved in various problem areas.

Thirdly, it sets out to be *a manifesto for action*. We are not helpless. There are many ways in which the individual can affect the behaviour of institutions and commercial organizations. In recent years, decisions of national importance have been influenced for the better by the efforts of determined individuals who have devoted time and energy to mobilizing public opinion.

Those are the three purposes of this book. But it is not a negative book. I am not arguing for a sterile other-worldliness, that we should keep our children wrapped in a cocoon, somehow insulating them from the twentieth century. I don't believe the Bible encourages this or even offers us the option, even if it were possible.

In this book we will be examining not just risks but also alternatives. We are living in an exciting environment. The children of today will grow up into a world very different from that in which we have lived. It will offer challenges and creative opportunities that we cannot imagine.

It is our plain duty as parents not just to protect our children from those who would damage them, but to help them to take advantage of, and enjoy, the good and exciting things that surround them.

First of all, then, some historical background.

Eleven years on

In 1974 I wrote a book called *The Media*.[1] Now long out of print, it was written for young people of around fifteen years old and upwards, and was intended to give some guidance, based on the Bible, for young people having problems relating their Christian faith to the world in which they lived. It dealt with such subjects as pop music, cinema, teenage magazines and other areas where Christians have often had problems.

Looking through it now, my immediate reaction is that while some things have changed dramatically in eleven years, others have not. The subjects that needed talking about still need talking about, and one of the encouragements about being a Christian today is the number of individuals, organizations and books that exist to help young people to live in a world which by and large has little interest in Christianity and does not create its social and cultural environment with a view to pleasing God.

But what strikes me very forcibly as I look at *The Media* is that there has been one shift of emphasis that is very relevant to the present book.

When I wrote in 1974, we were still in the heyday of the swinging sixties. The Beatles and the Mersey sound, the hippy movement, flower-power, *That Was The Week That Was*, new cults and religions, avant-garde cinema, Carnaby Street—though fading, they were all still comparatively recent. The Woodstock Music Festival, which had been a focus for the excitement of a generation, had happened only five years earlier.

Young people in 1974 were a significant lobby and a powerful buying elite. The fashions of the sixties, which had built Carnaby Street into the clothes capital of the West, had been the product of a society in which the young had money to spend. They had enough money to buy new clothes frequently, and to afford the sort of expensive garments that make the running in the fashion race.

Had we but realized it, we were already living in the twilight of that period. In Britain 1974 was the year of the miners' strike, seen by some commentators as the beginning of our most recent industrial troubles, for it ushered in a new era of confrontation between government and Trade Unions.

The spiral of inflation had already taken off; wages were beginning to fall behind prices.

By 1974, for the first time, unemployment had reached the one million mark. By 1976 it was to reach one and a third million, prices were to rise dramatically and wage settlements were to soar.

In 1974 the effect of these developments had not begun to bite. But as I write, over eleven years later, it can be seen in perspective.

In Liverpool, for example, where I was living, 1974 was for many young people a year of poetry and street theatre. Crowds came to public poetry readings, or attended dramatic events of all kinds. There was music in the streets of Toxteth and sometimes dancing in the parks. Not long before, American beat poet Allen Ginsberg had visited Liverpool and pronounced it 'the centre of the human consciousness of the universe'. The bulky, bearded American with the far-out ideas was still remembered affectionately in pubs near where I lived.

There was certainly no shortage of cash. I was at that time in my final year as a mature student at Liverpool University, but before then I had been in a job. It didn't pay especially well, but I had eaten out most nights of the week in the local bistro, had a flat of my own, and usually had enough left over to buy books and records, go to London occasionally, and even put some by for a rainy day. Most of my friends were working or students; only a few were on the dole.

In the mid-eighties, national unemployment in real terms approaches the four million mark, and Liverpool has changed.

Merseyside is among the hardest-hit areas of the country. Toxteth has seen some of the worst rioting and unrest that Britain has experienced in postwar years.

There is a massive drug problem among the young. In August 1985, the newspapers gave prominence to the death of a fourteen-year-old boy from heroin in one of the city's suburbs.[2]

Unemployment averages at least 20%, and among school-leavers stands at 42%.[3]

Somehow, the city still retains the magic that it once had. When I visit it from my home in the South of England it still seems to me to be one of the most exciting cities I have ever known. But it looks different. The shops are different. The young people don't have the sort of money any more that enables them to keep up-to-date with every fashion or music trend.

It's the same in Newcastle, in London, in Portsmouth, in Cardiff, in Glasgow, and in most of our cities. And it is the same in many of the rural areas; in the country towns, in the villages—and predominantly in the urban and rural north of the British Isles. Teenagers and under-thirties aren't a boom market any more. They are an economic and social disaster area.

If one were to write *The Media* in 1985 it would have to be written differently. The pressures on teenagers today are not primarily cultural but social. In many parts of the country, a Christian school-leaver is not likely to be wondering how he or she is going to cope with rock music so much as how life on the dole is to have any meaning or purpose.

Teenagers are no longer a buying elite. They no longer represent a market to be tapped in the way that manufacturers of everything from jeans to airline tickets rushed to sell their wares to them in the sixties.

But younger children are.

It's one of the strange though predictable results of a depression that one area where families economize last is in luxuries for the children. It's as though they are determined that however much the adults have to tighten their belts, the children won't suffer just because the family has no breadwinner.

Through the worst years of the recent depression, the toy market has flourished. Children are a strong market.

There are many differences between the mid-seventies and the mid-eighties, but this is one of the most significant: in the field of entertainment and luxury, the role of the young child has become increasingly important and that of the teenager and school-leaver less significant. Though the record industry, for example, is not by any means in its death-throes, and sales of popular music still subsidize those of classical music, it is not quite the boom industry it was. Whole new industries have developed purely because of this shift of emphasis, and old established ones traditionally selling into the younger children's market have flourished. Some industries selling into older teenage markets have extended their marketing appeal to the younger age groups.

This does not mean that the toy market, for example, is immoral. It does not mean that high-volume sales of toys are necessarily exploitative of the young. But it is one illustration of the fact that today children are the focus of attention for many interested parties. They are a source of untapped profits.

That means that the possibilities of exploitation exist. There is a risk.

Exploitation

We must be clear about what we mean by the word 'exploit-ation'. It's a word which has been often used lightly. There are certain toys, for example, which are currently enormous-ly popular with children. One example is the craze for futur-istic space robots and vehicles.

Two of the most popular are called 'Masters of the Uni-verse' and 'Convertors'. Both are TV spin-offs, models of fantastic constructions, weird dreams of centuries ahead and undreamed-of planets.

'Convertors' are mechanical robots, their box-covers illus-trated with pictures of them lumbering across lunar land-scapes. They 'convert' by springing apart to reveal an ar-moury of smaller weapons, vehicles and robots. Convertors are armies moving as a single unit.

'Masters of the Universe' likewise creates robots with extraordinary abilities. One toy that is being extensively advertised on television as I write is the 'Dragon Walker'. It is a very clever gadget indeed, which achieves forward move-ment by a combination of sliding and swivelling in a compli-cated progress unlike any other vehicle, real or imaginary.

The interesting thing about these toys is that they have absolutely no counterpart in real life. They are totally imaginary. Children have no reason for wanting to possess them apart from their own intrinsic fascination. They are also often expensive—some quite outside the average child's pocket money.

One could say that these manufacturers are exploiting children. The argument would run something like this: the manufacturer has created an essentially meaningless object which, by heavy promotion and extremely effective market-ing, is made irresistible to children.

A variety of pressures help this process. Peer group pres-sure, of course, is a very strong one. When all the kids in your class at school have a Dragon Walker, you want one too. Another pressure is the manufacturer's presentation of the product as part of a set—'Be the first to get them all' is a strong incentive to further acquisition.

Similar buying patterns apply to film spin-offs such as the *Star Wars* toys, and also to Barbie dolls and Sindy dolls.

Often such a market is said to be exploitative of children, in that it manipulates them into wanting and buying—either directly or through their parents—toys which they do not need and which they would not have wanted, had the manufacturers not mounted the campaign in the first place.

It *is* exploitation of a sort. But only in the sense that all marketing is. The essence of marketing anything is to create an innovative product and convince people that they need to buy it. Toys are a competitive market in which the lifetime of a product is notoriously short lived, and advertising is consequently intensive and high powered. Mattel's toys are reasonably well-made, well-designed items which absorb a child's interest; and so they sell.

But toys like this do not qualify for 'exploitation' in the negative sense in which we will be using the word in this book—the sense of 'unscrupulous benefiting from weakness' or even 'persuasion against the will'.

I personally wouldn't buy these toys for a child, but my reason is not that they are immoral. It is that most of the children I happen to know would, I suspect, not play with them for long and would soon abandon my expensive investment and look for some new novelty.

However, other children may well be different. I know of a family with three sons who have played with *Star Wars* toys for much longer than I would have thought probable.

Yet it's the very fact that I *can* make such decisions that is significant. I have the opportunity to control the extent to which advertising affects my child. I can talk the matter through with him or her. We have had many discussions in my family, for instance, on Sindy dolls, and have reached a compromise; Eleanor can spend some of her pocket money on dressing Sindy, but not as much as she would like. Currently we are having similar discussions about a toy series called My Little Pony—a set of plastic horses which I personally find repellingly sentimental but which certainly, for my daughter, seem to justify their cost in terms of play value.

'Exploitation', I would suggest, doesn't mean simply 'selling large quantities of toys to children (and to adults, on their behalf)'.

So what does it mean?

Cruelty and irresponsibility

The real danger to children exists in two main areas.

Firstly, where children are deliberately used for the profit and benefit of other people because they are too weak and defenceless to protect themselves. We shall be talking, for example, about drug abuse and sexual abuse. In these, adults are exploiting children by profiting from their weakness. This is cruelty.

Secondly, where children are exposed to influences which will harm them and in some cases destroy them, because those responsible for creating those influences cannot be bothered to establish adequate safeguards against children being affected. We shall, for example, be talking about the fantasy industry, where there is a shocking lack of safeguards and restrictions. This is irresponsibility.

Both are exploitation in its worst sense. Where it exists, all parents and adults who care for children's rights should be so concerned that they decide to protect those affected and challenge those responsible.

There are sometimes grey areas where the two merge. For example, certain brand dolls project a glamorous view of life which implies that happiness lies in the acquisition of worldly goods and that the best relationships involve jet-setting holidays, expensive riding garments, and all the other trappings of the fictional rich. The morality of influencing a child into a superficial and shallow view of life as part of a profit-making manufacturing operation is certainly open to doubt.

In this book we shall be looking at examples of cruelty and of irresponsibility.

Helping the children

In defending children against both of these, there is a great deal to be done on the individual and corporate level. And without doubt much is being done today.

One organization that has achieved a great deal in the protection of children is the National Society for the Prevention of Cruelty to Children (the NSPCC). It was founded in 1884, as part of the national stirring of conscience that resulted in the beginnings of the abolition of child labour, the Education Acts and other movements for child protection.

In 1889, Parliament passed an Act which was the first piece of legislation ever designed specifically to protect children: the 'Children's Charter'.

In May 1984 the Prime Minister addressed the Society as part of its centenary year celebrations. Speaking of the Society's role in the passing of the Children's Charter, she said:

> It was an achievement which owed much to two ideas. First that something had to be done; second that we had a personal responsibility to do it—we couldn't just leave it to the State. And so began the NSPCC.[4]

The thrust of her speech was an appeal to adults to adopt the same responsibility:

> I was interested to read very recently about a survey carried out in the EEC which found that two thirds of the adult population of the Community think that parents nowadays spend too little time with their children. And when it came to arrangements for giving them more time together, fathers were just as interested as mothers. . . .

She finished with a challenge:

> Children are the hope of the future, but they are also people of the present. They are people whose lives are a gift to us, whose development is our responsibility, whose protection and well-being are our duty. Where else can they turn, if not to us?

Real cruelty to children happens when that responsibility is rejected.

Conclusion

The conditions that existed in England when the NSPCC was founded have mercifully disappeared. We no longer condemn children to a middle age of lung disease and other fatal illness by sending them up chimneys when they are tiny. No longer does a child have to operate a loom, pick coal in a mine, or spend long hours at a workbench.

Why then do the NSPCC and organizations like it still exist?

Because although some abuses have gone, others remain and new ones have arrived. In its 1983 *Annual Report*, the NSPCC stated: '[It is] unthinkable that our work should ever come to an end while there are thousands upon thousands of children who need our help.'

The Royal Charter of the Society states that its purpose is 'to prevent the public and private wrongs of children and the corruption of their morals'. In the 1984 *Annual Report* that purpose was re-emphasized:

> The problems facing children today are a tragic reflection of today's troubled society, with the greater incidence of divorce and remarriage, the increasing number of young mothers, and high levels of unemployment all taking their toll.[5]

A report published by the NSPCC in December 1985 revealed that at least one child dies each week in Britain at the hands of parents or relatives.

There are many organizations besides the NSPCC that

directly or indirectly work for the wellbeing of children. The Nationwide Festival of Light, for example, produced a leaflet[6] that set out four 'simple basic rights for all children'. These are:

1. The right of every child to be born (referring to the abortion situation in Britain).
2. The right of every child to the care of its natural mother and father in a family setting.
3. The right to be treated as a child (referring to commercial exploitation).
4. The right to be introduced to God.

Another organization very active in this area is CARE Trust, founded in 1983 as a successor to the Nationwide Festival of Light. The Trust's 'mandate for the 1980s' reads:

> To encourage and promote biblical and Christian action, research and education in order to support the integrity of the family, the centrality of marriage, and the sanctity of human life from conception.

> To encourage those Christians already working in these fields, and to provide research and resource material to help them.

> To encourage every Christian throughout Britain to understand the issues facing society, and the place of the church in Christ-like caring.

> To train Christians in basic caring skills, and to encourage professionals to work out how biblical insights affect their work.[7]

In November 1985 the Chairman of CARE Campaigns wrote: 'We believe 1985 has laid the base for an effective evangelical voice on a political level in this country and that 1986 and 1987 will confirm what power that evangelical voice is to have.'[8]

Another organization that has become increasingly involved in this field is the Evangelical Alliance. While primarily an alliance of churches, denominations, para-church societies and individuals, the EA encourages its member bodies (which include CARE Trust and *Family* magazine) and draws on the concern of the broad evangelical constituency.

Other organizations will be mentioned as we go on, and further details and addresses can be found in the Notes at the end of the book.

Besides organizations, some periodicals have a special concern for children's needs. A Christian magazine, *Family*, has monitored progress for a considerable time now in several crucial areas and has been involved in some significant campaigns, as for example its action, with the Evangelical Alliance, to restrict children's access to some parts of the London Dungeon, a commercial chamber of horrors.[9] The *Daily Mail* has taken a particular interest in social issues affecting the welfare of children, and its television preview criticism is often extremely helpful for parents wanting to plan their family viewing ahead.

In this book I have been necessarily selective. For example, I have chosen to talk about child sexual abuse rather than child abuse in general, because the facts about the former are so alarming and so little known. I have included children's books, but only fantasy role-playing books; there are many studies of children's literature in general from a biblical viewpoint, but the fantasy books are a very recent development. In a quite lengthy discussion of television, I have said relatively little about televised violence, because that is a topic that has had a great deal of coverage already.[10]

The chapter titles should not therefore be taken as an exhaustive survey of the subject, nor a guide to the areas that are most disturbing or most dangerous. They are intended to be a representative selection to illustrate problems. Sadly, there are many more areas not covered in this book.

However, the same general guidelines apply in every case, both those included and those left out.

1. Children are vulnerable, and need our protection.
2. It is possible to have freedom in our daily lives for ourselves and our children—but it involves caring about what our children are experiencing, and accepting the extra work that this sometimes involves.
3. We do not need to wrap our children in cotton wool. Childhood is a time of *protection* and *preparation*. It is our task to introduce them to the world, without allowing them to be crushed by it.

It's a privilege—and a responsibility.

2

Television

We have neighbours, good friends of ours, who for several years did not own a television. They are a family with two children; the husband is a potter.

Life without television was rich and full. They spent a good deal of time with the children; read to them, did craft of various kinds, went walking in the country, talked to each other, and enjoyed their home and their friends.

Perhaps this is beginning to sound like a fable with an obvious moral—'Then they got a television and everything fell to pieces—they stopped talking to each other, turned into vegetables and sat in front of the television every evening like zombies.'

But that wasn't what happened. They did get a television, a colour set which was given to them by a relative. And they didn't put it away in a remote spare room upstairs, but found a place for it in a corner of the living room.

And they spend a good deal of time with the children, and read to them, do craft of various kinds, go walking in the country, talk to each other, and enjoy their family and friends.

And sometimes, they watch television.

I tell this story because it is one of the happiest examples that I know of the fact that television need not be a threat to family life.

For my neighbours, television has become a source of information when needed, a useful help in teaching their children about the human and natural world in which they live, and entertainment which is available when they choose to make use of it.

It does not put their children at risk. On the contrary, it expands their world and plays a significant part in the education process, besides taking its place alongside books, toys, games and other forms of entertainment.

It may seem like an ideal—the sort of thing you would expect in a potter's family living in an English village.

But it is not. It is simply a demonstration of the fact that television can be controlled, and assimilated into the life of a family without changing it for the worse.

Some statistics

It must be said that the odds are against this happening. Television has acquired a much more demanding place in our national life. The statistics speak for themselves. In the first quarter of 1984, for example, the average weekly time spent watching television in the United Kingdom was 21·75 hours per week for men and 25·5 hours for women.[1] In other words, an average of just over three hours a day for men and three and a half for women.

These figures do vary. People watch less television in the summer than in the winter, and the old watch more than the young. But in practical terms the fact is that Mr and Mrs Average, if they sit down in front of the television at seven each evening, do not leave it until well after ten.

Even more striking are the viewing figures for particular programmes. On July 9th 1984, 13·7 million people tuned in to that evening's episode of *Coronation Street*.[2] The population of the United Kingdom at the time was 56 million. Making due allowances for age and locality, that means that at least a quarter of the people in Britain watched that episode of *Coronation Street*.

Ted Harrison, a radio presenter, has calculated that each week we as a nation put in as many man-hours watching soap opera as it took medieval builders to build a cathedral.[3]

In the twenty-four hours of the working day, an employed adult sleeps an average of eight hours, works for eight hours, and has about eight hours left for leisure, meals, housework, travelling and so on. The hours devoted entirely to leisure and relaxation are probably about four.

The implications of such figures are thought-provoking. They mean that the majority of the time available for a family to be together is consumed, in most families, by television.

Nor do these figures apply only to a small part of the population. In 1983, only 2% of households had no television, 81% had colour sets, and 18% had video recorders—a rapidly increasing figure.[4]

Whatever we as a population are doing with all those televisions, we certainly don't seem to be turning them off very often!

Television and the family

If television assumes that kind of importance in a home, and is often switched on, there are a number of consequences for children.

1. Television teaches by reinforcement

For the very young, *television becomes part of the furniture, a part of the world about which they are learning*.

Children learn by reinforcement. An event that happens several times is increasingly interpreted as a fixed point in the child's universe. In the first steps of learning to feed himself, a baby will grab food that is too hot; after doing so several times, he will understand something about heat and the cooling process!

Similarly, before a child learns to talk he goes through a 'babbling' phase, in which he continually utters incomprehensible sounds and syllables. The parents' reaction of pleasure and understanding, when a pattern of sounds resembles a real word, helps the child to eliminate those noises which do not belong to speech. Later, the parents' constant repetition of the names of objects, while showing the objects to the child, will once more reinforce the learning process.[5]

In a home where television is often switched on in the early evening, it can easily become another source of data, operating by reinforcement.

Of course, in the earliest days, a child does not even understand what television is. A very young baby will often ignore the television completely, and be unable to make sense of the objects portrayed; most parents have been frustrated, as we ourselves were, by their baby's refusal to acknowledge the presence of another baby on the television.

As the child grows, however, and becomes able to recognize that the images on the screen have a meaning, he associates the televised image with reality. If he sees a film of a space station he assumes that the space station actually exists somewhere. This is why children are often easily frightened by obvious caricatures and comic figures on television. They cannot understand that it's only a joke.

The final stage in the development of what Patricia Greenfield has called 'television literacy'[6] comes when the child realizes that the televised representation is not necessarily reality, but that it might very well become reality. A killing in a cowboy film may be accepted as pure fantasy, but nevertheless the child's response includes an awareness that people do get killed in real life and that it might happen to anybody.

In short, television becomes an example. It presents to the child images which he understands as at least comparable to the world in which he lives, and by presenting the images on a regular basis it reinforces them.

If you watch a group of children playing cowboys and Indians (or spacemen and aliens, or whatever), you will see players who are supposed to have been killed die in a 'television' way—melodramatic, with lots of writhing and arching of the back. Their idea of what happens when somebody dies comes from television. They have seen it happen so many times that they accept it. They have acquired that 'knowledge' from TV.

A more distressing example of learning by reinforcement is the increasing use of young children as humorous foils to older brothers and sisters in situation comedy. Imported American sitcom is particularly prone to this. *Diff'rent Strokes, Family Ties* and many more, show young children being worldly-wise about the activities of their elders. The studio audience roars with laughter as the child makes knowing comments about an older brother or sister staying out at night, or some other situation that offers the chance of sexual innuendo.

How many children, one wonders, are receiving week by week the message that to gain adult admiration and applause, that is the kind of worldly-wise cynicism that is required?

2. Television uses up time

It not only occupies the child, it occupies the parents as well. So the child's available time for other ways of getting to know the world—books, pictures, playing outside, talking to people—is diminished; but so is the limited time that a parent has to spend with a child.

While the child is watching television, and especially while the whole family watches together, the parents are in effect handing over to television the task of educating and bringing him up.

The loss of time has repercussions. A favourite programme can be planned for, but often something interesting will appear unexpectedly and play havoc with mealtimes or other activities that have been planned.

Often the television is switched on for one programme and is left on afterwards, and a programme is watched more out of inertia than interest. Sometimes it is used to 'unwind', when a member of the family comes home tired from work.

In some homes, television is used as a pacifier. If one of the children is demanding, the television is turned on and the child dumped in front of it. Much Saturday morning television is designed as a non-stop entertainment for bored kids (though there are some excellent holiday programmes, such as BBC1's aptly named *Why Don't You . . . Just Switch Off Your Television Set And Do Something Less Boring Instead?*).

Time is an expensive commodity in most homes. If the official statistics are correct, then a great deal of it is being allocated to television.

3. Television sets up its own loyalties

All parents try to bring up their children according to some idea of how they would like their children to behave. Christian parents, for example, have a very precise agenda for their children. They will want them to accept certain views of themselves and the world—to accept the good news of the gospel of Jesus Christ—and also to develop certain ways of behaving and of relating to other people.

For example, they will hope that their children will grow up honest, fair-minded, courageous, and unashamed of their faith.

They will also hope that their children will be considerate to other people, compassionate, charitable and, should they marry, faithful to their partners. They will hope that their children will not grow up to use foul language, to be sexually or racially bigoted, or to be dependent on drugs, tobacco or alcohol.

And in most of these the Christian parent is no different from hundreds of thousands of others.

The clearest teaching we can give our children is by example. How often have we come across an angry or unruly child, wondered how he or she became like it, then met the parents and immediately understood! As we have already seen, children learn by reinforcement. If a child sees foul language go unpunished every day at home, that child will find it very difficult to avoid growing up like his parents in that respect.

Our responsibility is to be clear and good examples to those whose young lives we influence. As Christian parents, we must model Jesus to them. And it is precisely at this point of awesome responsibility and privilege that television's demands upon a child's loyalty become apparent; for television has a quite different agenda.

At many points the two agendas coincide. For example, in the realm of ideas and attitudes television has an important role as a critic of society and a social conscience. As I write this, the soap opera *Brookside* has a storyline about a mentally disturbed man, with a grievance against the Hospital Service, who shoots a black nurse. Important issues about hospital overcrowding and understaffing, the Press, and racial prejudice are being raised and sympathetically discussed.

In major documentaries and in numerous magazine programmes, television does an invaluable job of informing and challenging. One outstanding area is that of the physically and mentally handicapped; for example, television does an astonishing amount for the deaf, both in running special programmes using broadcasters trained in sign-language, and in providing services such as the subtitles for major programmes available on teletext.

Another area in which television shares the agenda of anybody anxious to bring their children up to be understanding of other points of view is minority interests. BBC1's *Black and White Media Show* was an unassuming but profoundly provocative study of racial prejudice. Channel 4's *Black on Black* was a forum for ethnic minority interest groups. *Gharbar,* again on BBC1, is a magazine programme for

Asian viewers. In the case of many of these programmes Christians should give a hearty welcome to them.

In these and in other issues television is, by and large, a powerful ally in the task of parenthood.

But at the level of behaviour, language and personal morals, television's different agenda is clear. It has no brief to bring your child up as a Christian or even as a good citizen. Its brief is to serve the needs of its public, and thereby it reflects whatever the prevailing standards are.

The result is that two examples can easily compete in your home. On one hand, there is the example you set your children; on the other, the example that television sets. It is frustrating in the extreme when you try to teach by your own example, if that example is constantly being contradicted by another.

One of the most often discussed aspects of television is its portrayal of violence. A 1972 study, for example, suggested that there was a direct link between schoolchildren watching televised violence and their level of acceptance of violence as a way of dealing with problems.[7] In 1985 Lord Lane, the Lord Chief Justice, claimed that 'thanks to TV and quite often thanks to TV news reporting, violence is self-perpetuating.'[8] This is all the more disturbing in view of the evidence that television is becoming an increasingly strong influence on children's outlooks.

But more alarming, because more insidious, is the lowering of standards in what is considered acceptable family television. Let me give two examples. *Bottle Boys* was a situation comedy set in a dairy. The Bottle Boys were milkmen. The show went out on Saturday evenings at 7.15 pm—peak family viewing time ('family viewing time' officially extends to 9 pm). Thousands of families watch it together.

On August 3rd 1985 the plot revolved around a competition to find the milkman who could sell the most chickens on his round. But the secondary plot was entirely based on the sexual adventures of the milkmen (incidentally incorporating an ugly stereotype of housewives as being bored empty-headed dolls ready to leap into bed with any passing tradesman). This secondary plot was what the final comical outcome depended on, and the script frequently used the subject for raising laughs from the audience.

The Benny Hill Show is a TV favourite that reappears year after year. It features quick-fire sketches with little dialogue. It is well-known for its scantily-clad dancers who choreograph very explicit sexual gestures into their dances. The show is highly destructive towards women—who are treated as sex objects throughout—uses foreign accents (particularly Chinese) as a source of fun, and makes promiscuity and adultery the basis of most of its humour. A nasty twist in *The Benny Hill Show* is that sexual encounters are often between young, pretty girls and old men.

Of course the response to such a description of shows like these is often: 'Oh, you're taking it much too seriously! It's good fun, slapstick; nobody minds.'

But the effect of such a show is to reinforce week by week Hill's attitudes. Each week the audience waits eagerly for his stereotype of the bespectacled, grinning Chinese visitor who cannot make himself understood because of his accent, and each week the idea is reinforced that Chinese people are comical, rather stupid and speak in an entertaining way.

The price of freedom

Those are three ways in which television has an effect on children. They are all potential risk areas. But if that is so, then how can television be used as a positive factor in the home?

I believe that the key to doing so is that one has to work at it.

If television has a part to play in reinforcing a child's learning, then it can be turned to useful purpose. It would be quite possible to put together a list of programmes which could be the basis of an exciting project which you and your child could do together.

A project on 'The Sea', for example, might make use of a cartoon about deep sea diving and adventures in the ocean depths; a travel film might give an opportunity to find out some facts and figures; a showing of *Robinson Crusoe* or *Swiss Family Robinson* might give an excellent chance to find out about surviving on the sea's resources.

There are dozens of ways in which similar projects can be devised. And it achieves another valuable result; it makes television into a 'doing' thing, not just a 'watching' thing.

So far as the use of time is concerned, the aim must be to decrease the amount of time spent watching television and increase that spent together doing other things. To do this without losing the good things that television offers means careful planning. The *Radio Times* and *TV Times* are essential reading for anybody who takes family television seriously, because they enable you to plan your viewing. It is often a good idea to note the time of a programme in your family diary. If it's a film or feature programme, why not make it special—have supper round the television, pull the chairs around in a cosy semi-circle?

After the programme, switch the set off. Then talk together about the programme. Discuss it, argue about it. Interact with what you have seen, and as a family share your thoughts and opinions.

This will serve two purposes.

First, it will protect the child from going away alone—possibly to bed—with images in his mind that may be distressing and disturbing. If the programme turned out to be frightening, now is the chance to talk it through.

Secondly, it will give you, the parent, the opportunity to challenge the programme's assumptions. If there has been a vivid portrayal of violence, if statements have been made attacking Christianity, if foul language has been used, or if a sexual encounter has been explicitly portrayed that you had not realized would be part of the programme—now is the time to talk it through as a family and to share with your children your views on the matters as a Christian. You may want to have a Bible within reach. It might be appropriate to pray together before you finish. No doubt you will find the way of doing things that suits you best as a family.

And finally there is the issue of television's own agenda, the example it sets.

I believe very strongly that television should never be left on as background. As a family we never have the news on unless we are able to listen to it properly. It is just too easy to desensitize oneself by repeatedly hearing accounts of war, suffering and death.

In a different way the same applies to any television programme. Because so much of television, and especially light comedy shown at supposedly 'family' viewing hours, carries sexual innuendo, swearing, blasphemy and racial and sexist bigotry, children cannot be left to watch it uncritically.

Your *Radio Times* and *TV Times* are your best helps here. These will give you quite a good idea of what a programme will be like, and you can plan ahead to avoid programmes which you know to be unsuitable.

It may be that following such a plan will change your viewing habits dramatically. But I think it is well worth it. There is a sense in which what is important is not so much the programmes you allow your children to see, but the fact that they know that a process of choice is going on.

When your children leave the family and set up their own homes, you will not be helping them very much if you simply give them as they leave a list of television programmes that they must not watch. Apart from anything else, lists get out of date, so your help would be short-lived.

But if, having shared for several years in the choosing of what you will watch together as a family, they leave with an understanding of why as a Christian you made the choices you did, then they will be able to go on and make their own choices.

It takes time and commitment. It's actually much easier just to dump a fractious child in front of the television and retreat gratefully. But to protect your child, to be able to say of your seven-year-old that you know exactly which programmes she has watched that week, and to be involved with your fourteen-year-old in learning discrimination and wisdom in making choices, is hard work.

The results are worth it. Television has much to offer a child. As Christians we have great freedom. But, as it always has been, the price of freedom is eternal vigilance!

The open door

The late-night feature film was *Carrie*, a disturbing horror film about a girl who, with the onset of puberty, discovers that she can move objects by merely exerting her will. The film ends in a horrific climax, as objects fly in all directions and a massive fire breaks out. Earlier she has killed her cruel mother by piercing her with hooked knives, a grotesque death that is photographed in lurid detail.

Much more disturbing than the physical violence is the psychological horror. The film begins with Carrie, who is aged about thirteen, naked in the school showers. She begins menstruating for the first time, and having been told nothing by her mother is quite unprepared. She is hysterical with fright, the other girls howl ridicule and contempt at her, and the camera records every moment with quite unnecessary visual detail. Throughout the film, sexual maturity and sexual relationships are equated with trauma and horror.

I have often wondered what the effect of that film would have been on, say, an eleven-year-old boy who chanced to see it. Would it be his first awareness of female physiology? How much would he know about sex anyway? Would he have ever seen a girl naked? If not, what sort of subconscious revulsions would he acquire, as a result of seeing *Carrie* late at night, when his mind was at its least resisting, and when several hours sleep straight afterwards would prevent any further experiences diluting the impact of the film?

It does not take very much imagination to envisage him having real marital problems later on as a result of that one night's viewing, and one wonders how many counsellors have to sort out problems in adults caused by similar experiences in their clients when children.

It is not an impossible story, and it illustrates another risk element in television. Television is an open door. It brings into the home the cinema and the rock concert, the sports field and the stage. Some of these are not at all suitable for children.

This is not television's fault. It is not a service entirely for children, so its responsibility towards them where such films are concerned lies in scheduling potentially harmful material outside the hours when children could safely be expected to be in bed. (The broadcasting authorities then have a responsibility to adults, who might well also have something to say about such films.)

So how can we best protect our children from accidental traumas like the one I have described?

First and foremost, of course—no late night television!

It sounds obvious, but there can be unintended problems. For example, some programmes screened after 9 pm are ones one might want to allow a child to watch; live sport, State occasions, a programme about a part of the world that the family has visited together—there are many perfectly acceptable programmes for which a child might be allowed to stay up late on a special occasion.

But in the warm, cuddly atmosphere of the fireside it is very tempting to let the television run on in the background after the programme, to others which are not at all suitable for young children. The child, half asleep, is least well equipped in such circumstances to resist any distress or confusion. The images will be taken back to bed where they may well cause nightmares sooner or later.

A similar problem can arise when a child wakes up late at night and needs comfort. The parents may be watching a programme which would damage a child. It's very easy to cuddle him while continuing to watch the programme over his shoulder. So he goes back to bed with gunshots, or screams, or violence, or other distress fresh in his mind, and the result is the same.

It takes a conscious decision to switch the set off and concentrate on the needs of one's son or daughter. My own children invariably pick the cliff-hanging moment, or the part of the film that contains the vital clue, in which to wake up!

Secondly, one needs to be aware that sometimes films and programmes appear on television, often earlier in the day, which can be damaging for other reasons.

Children can be damaged not just by witnessing sex and violence but by barely understood reality, and potentially disturbing films are often presented in the middle of the evening. In the current *Radio Times* as I write, for example, there is a factual programme about the likelihood of earthquakes in Naples (8 pm) and a play about Northern Ireland (9.05 pm).

I am not for a moment arguing that plays about sectarian killings in Northern Ireland or films about earthquake devastation ought not to be broadcast in case children see them (though certainly it's the responsibility of every concerned viewer to watch such programmes critically and when necessary express an opinion to the broadcasting authorities). What I am saying is that we can't simply draw a line across the programme schedules at a certain time of day and relax knowing that anything before that line is 'safe' for a particular child to watch.

Our responsibility to our children to know what they are watching wherever possible includes ensuring that a particular child does not see a programme for which he or she may not be ready. This may mean that a small child, allowed to watch one early evening programme with the family, will have to be taken away from the television while his older brothers and sisters are allowed to go on watching the one that follows; the younger child may not be ready for the level of excitement or tension which is acceptable for older children. In families with children of widely differing ages it is all too easy to forget that the child that sat entranced watching *Dr Dolittle* is still sitting there, watching a wartime documentary or some other item for which he or she is not ready.

For example, the series of anti-bomb films that marked the Hiroshima anniversary were well worth showing. Whatever one's views on nuclear weapons, everybody should know what the effects of nuclear war are and the suffering that innocent civilians invariably undergo. That is our responsibility, as adults, to the dead and dying of Hiroshima and Nagasaki.

Whether it is also our responsibility as parents to show them indiscriminately to children is debatable. Adults have a buffer of reason which filters television and prevents the full emotional impact from affecting them. It is the achievement of many anti-bomb films that they have substantially penetrated that buffer, but it exists.

A child does not have the buffer in the same way. There will come a time for every child when he or she will be ready to see such films, and at that time it may be appropriate for an older child to be allowed to stay up late and afterwards talk about what has been seen with his or her parents.

Choosing that time is a delicate matter. Only the parents will really be able to judge whether it has arrived or not. The broadcasting authorities certainly can't, nor should they be expected to. It is our responsibility, and it is hard work.

And thirdly, it's important, once more, to look at the schedules in advance and know what is coming on television.

The *Radio Times* and *TV Times* give detailed outlines and feature articles; most daily newspapers have advance reviews of programmes. In the case of films, a reference book that I have found useful for my own needs is *Halliwell's Film Guide*.[9] Leslie Halliwell is a television film buyer, and his book gives details of hundreds of films together with capsule reviews. It covers about 80% of the films that appear on television.

If you have problems as a family in arranging your viewing so that programmes which adults want to see don't clash with the needs of the family to be together and the needs of children not to be unnecessarily distressed, it's worth considering buying or renting a video recorder.

That can open up some new problems, such as video addiction, but it can make a great difference to one's pattern of viewing—a difference for the better.

The half-open door

So far, I have argued that a major part of the responsibility in ensuring that television is a benefit to our homes and not a threat lies with parents.

If you have an open door in your home, through which anybody or anything can come, it's sensible to set some sort of a watchdog to see who or what is coming through the door. As parents, we are the watchdogs.

An open door is in many ways relatively easy to deal with. You know the door is open. You know that what is liable to come through it may be dangerous. You know what is necessary to 'close the door'—if you have done your watching well, it is easy to switch the set off beforehand.

Much less easy to deal with is the half-open door.

Television is in fact much more of a half-open door than an open one. The problem lies in the fact that its function is to reflect our society by providing entertainment and information that will be acceptable to as many people as possible. It is not a medium that is well suited to lost causes and tiny minorities. Channel 4, for example, caters for such interests but is itself a minority channel (in July 1984 it was watched on average for ten minutes per day, and attracted only 6% of the total television audience[10]).

Television occupies the centre ground in the media. It tends to absorb the topics it discusses into a generalized neutrality. Though many programmes exist which are sharply individualistic, the programme planners have a right and a duty to ensure that the overall balance is acceptable to a broad constituency.

Immediately the Christian has a problem. Though we live in a country that is still nominally Christian, with freedom of worship taken for granted as a basic human right, our society is not a Christian society any longer. If a visitor from outer space, for instance, tried to work out from our behaviour and our daily newspapers what the British view of marriage and the family is, he would have to conclude that we think them of very little importance.

We are not a nation that places a very high practical value on compassion; divided between a rich South and a poor North, with four million unemployed, we have made little real progress towards a fair and just society. We are capable of great generosity and selflessness, as was seen in the response to Bob Geldof's appeals for help for the starving in Africa which he launched in 1984. But by and large we muddle along with the status quo, because the weak have little power to change things and the strong are comfortable as they are—and successive governments have not been able to change us.

The gospel stands against cruelty, insensitivity, greed, and injustice. The Bible shines a light on the world and criticizes what it exposes. And Jesus has always been 'despised and rejected of men'.

So a television that mirrors a society such as ours cannot help but daily present many things which as Christians we must stand against as well.

Through the half-open door, for example, comes racial

stereotyping. Our children are constantly fed material which presents other nationalities as in some way inferior to our own. Much of it comes through old films being reshown, and are really the attitudes of a previous generation. But much of it also comes through present-day productions.

It's a reinforcement, an education into prejudice.

Lenny Henry, the black comedian, has said[11] that he regrets his earlier material which used the colour of his skin for cheap laughs. When he first appeared on television he exploited all the clichés of white prejudice—rolling his eyes, wearing war paint, deliberately affecting that thick African accent that few blacks actually have but which is stock-in-trade for the clubland comic. Nowadays, he says, he is looking for common ground, a contribution to humour that is uniquely black-conceived but which is not exploitative.

Through the same half-open door comes a view of life that is starved and miserable. In many soap operas, for example, greed is the motivation for the plot, relationships are characterized by bitterness and deceit, and there is no religious dimension to life at all.

What is the effect of a weekly diet of *Dallas* and *Dynasty*? What example is it giving to children of how the world operates?

In its projection of a world of incredible wealth, sexual conniving, and soured relationships, *Dallas,* for example, is reinforcing the notion that success in this world means material success, something so desirable that trampling on other people is a legitimate way of achieving it.

A general lowering of everyday standards comes through the door. Think of the kind of language that is taken for granted in much light entertainment and in more serious television.

Schoolmaster Charles Oxley's experiment in Lancashire, when he set his pupils to counting the obscenities in television programmes, caught the imagination of the Press and was widely ridiculed. But his point was valid. In almost every comedy show on television, swearing is accepted as normal. Gradually the child, by regular reinforcement, is fed the idea that the way to react to shock, surprise, or even pleasure, is to swear.

The door is only half open. You cannot stand with a hand on the switch, ready to turn the television set off as soon as somebody swears. You can't scrutinize the schedules to try to work out how ruthless J. R. Ewing is going to be that week.

It's in these areas where television is often insensitive to the fact that children do watch adult programmes.

It is disgraceful that at 7.15 pm on a Saturday evening *Bottle Boys* should create comedy about adulterous milkmen.

It is quite unacceptable that a comedy such as *Are You Being Served?* should feature a running joke about camp homosexuality. Whatever view one takes of homosexuality, it is not a matter for cheap jokes. When the time comes for me to explain to my children what homosexuality is, I don't want it to be because they want to know why everybody laughs when Mr Humphries says, 'I'm free.'

One could go on. There are hundreds of similar examples.

Action

So what can we do?

I want to emphasize that we are not confined to a passive role in television, and we are not confined to simply finding out when we should switch off and when it is likely to be safe to switch on, though that is useful knowledge and we should try to acquire it.

Television is a marketplace. Its product relies on public acceptance. Viewing figures matter. Television authorities listen.

And so I would like to propose an agenda for action, using ideas which have been introduced by many people in the past—I do not claim any originality for them.

1. In the home

(a) Be aware. It is vital that you know what your children are watching. At home, we make it a rule not to allow any programme to be watched that is an unknown quantity to us. We sit and watch the first episode of a new series together, and decide afterwards whether or not to allow the programme to be watched again.

Hopefully, we are never in the situation of not knowing whether our eight-year-old child is watching something unhelpful or not.

It takes up time, and it can cause tears, if a child becomes attached to a programme which after the first viewing you decide isn't one you want him or her to see. But it's the first step, I believe, in helping children to benefit from television.

(b) Encourage interaction. Early evening television programmes for children are often excellent (but please don't take my word for it, check them out for yourselves!). In several cases they maintain the high standards set by the old much-missed radio *Children's Hour*.

Most of them have some form of interaction—the children are encouraged to involve themselves in musical items, sing-songs, making models, and answering questions.

Encourage your children to take part. One of the most rewarding experiences is to enter a room where a young child is watching television alone and find the child singing along with the presenter, calling out answers to questions, and interacting with what is going on.

Conversely, one of the saddest things to see is a child staring at a television set, watching other children on the screen doing things, and remaining uninvolved himself.

(c) Limit viewing. Television is a little like eating chocolate; it is difficult sometimes to convince a child that he should stop. A firm hand on the on/off switch will not only protect your child, it will make time available for other things. The fact that many early evening programmes are

very good does not mean that your child should watch them all; it simply gives you a wider choice.

(d) Don't make the television the most exciting toy in the house. If you have a large set, consider changing it for a smaller one. In any case, if it presently occupies a central position in your living room, dethrone it!

When you do not have the television on, make sure that the children do not miss it.

A friend of mine with three children used to set aside the time between the children coming home from school and suppertime, for craft with the children. She prepared supper beforehand and when the children arrived she had paints, paper, paste, scissors and all sorts of interesting projects ready for them.

She did this because she was not prepared to hand over her children to the television for what she believed to be a most important hour in the day. She was not critical of children's television; she simply saw it as a poor second-best.

It took forward planning and lots of energy to do as she did. But the children enjoyed their special time with her so much that there would have been a chorus of protest if she had switched the television on instead!

(e) Consider whether you should get rid of the television. I have left this until last, because I personally believe that television is much better inside the home than outside it. Inside your family it can be part of the child's growing up, and the decisions you make together will help to teach your children that decisions are important, and how to make them. If you have no television, you might be bequeathing your children a major problem in learning how to handle it when they have left home and you are not there to guide them.

However, in some situations, for a variety of reasons, the sensible course of action is to get rid of the set. Before you do so, consider changing to a portable and putting it somewhere in the house that is rarely used for family living. If you get rid of it completely, you can expect to gain some considerable advantages, but you will have to work rather harder to replace the good things that television offers—particularly knowledge of travel and the natural world, which television usually presents superbly.

2. Outside the home

(a) Write to the producers. If you have particularly enjoyed a programme, write and say so. Conversely, if you are offended or upset by a programme, write and say so as well. Remember, viewers' opinions *are* taken seriously, especially when courteously and convincingly expressed.

(i) Write a concise letter. Don't make general comments on the state of broadcasting today—give as precise details as you can (if complaining) of what it was that annoyed you.

(ii) Be courteous, and make sure that you understand what it was that the programme was attempting to do. If you are complaining that a programme was unsuitable for family viewing, remember that the Independent Broadcasting Authority defines family viewing as viewing before 9 pm.

(iii) Address your letter to: The Producer, [Name of the programme], and then the national BBC or regional ITV company concerned. The address of BBC Television is: Lime Grove, Shepherd's Bush, London W12, telephone 01-743 8000. The address of your regional ITV company can be obtained from your local library (ask them to check in *Whitaker's Almanack*), or in such publications as CARE Trust's leaflet *To Praise or to Blame,* or Mrs Mary Whitehouse's book *Mightier than the sword.*[12]

(iv) Write as soon as possible after the programme. If you would like to telephone, ask for the Duty Officer and make your point briefly.

(b) Take every opportunity of representing your point of view on television. Right to Reply (Channel 4) has been justly praised for its fairness and openness to criticism from viewers. Such programmes as BBC1's *Points of View,* while often trivializing the points made, are an opportunity to make an opinion known, and there are others. It can encourage other people to make their voices heard if you take the first step. The points made above about courtesy and conciseness still apply.

(c) Write to the governing bodies. Where you need to appeal to the highest possible authority, write to the governing bodies. These have a statutory responsibility to protect the public interest.[13]

Addresses are:

Mr Stuart Young, Chairman of the Governors, BBC, Broadcasting House, London W1A 1AA.

Lord Thomson, Independent Broadcasting Authority, 70 Brompton Road, London SW3 1EY.

Mr Jeremy Isaacs, Channel 4 Television Company, 60 Charlotte Street, London W1P 2AX.

(d) Link up with other Christians. The National Viewers and Listeners Association, The Order of Christian Unity, and several other organizations have campaigned on broadcasting. Addresses can be found in, for example, *UK Christian Handbook* (MARC Europe).

In any case, bring the matter before prayer groups and fellowship meetings in your church, and pray a great deal.

There are so many good and exciting things offered by television that will give your child enjoyment, education and information, that it would be tragic if the harmful and dangerous aspects of it should go unchallenged and unchecked.

3

Film

If television is a problem for a Christian parent, cinema is a lesser problem in at least one sense; while television thrives, the role of cinema in our national life is declining. In 1947, a questionnaire circulated to all the area's Head Teachers by the Northampton County Borough Education Committee revealed the following cinema attendance figures. Of the 1,411 pupils in the Grammar and Technical High Schools, 398 attended cinemas once a week, 97 twice a week, and 20 three times a week. Of the 1,153 pupils in Secondary Modern Schools, 974 attended one, 459 two, 104 three, 31 four, and 4 five times a week. Of the 7,579 pupils attending Primary Schools, 1,830 attended one, 500 two, 104 three, 40 four and 7 five times a week.[1]

In Britain there were about 4,750 cinemas selling between 25 and 30 million seats a week. In a Social Survey of that year it was shown that of the sixteen-to-nineteen-year-old age group, seven out of ten attended the cinema once a week or more frequently; of the ten-to-fifteen-year-old age group, 65% attended once a week or more frequently, and 30% attended occasionally. It was estimated that 25% of the total cinema audience was made up of children still of school age.

In 1983, the number of cinema screens in Britain was 1,293 (the number of cinema buildings being only 707).[2] The reason for the decline in numbers of cinemas and in attendances (now down to 1·2 million per week) is given as

> competition from television viewing, the rapid rise in the use of home video cassette recorders, with feature and other films available for low cost purchase or hire, and the effect of the economic recession on the spending power of a predominantly young cinema-going public.[3]

In 1947 the Saturday morning picture show—the Children's Cinema Club—was a regular highlight of the week for hundreds of thousands of children, and provided films of good quality which were scrutinized by the British Film Institute and other bodies. Today, only about 100 cinemas have Saturday morning showings.

At the same time, there is a resurgence in the British film industry. Many major American-financed films are made in England—*Star Wars* was one—and British films such as *Gandhi* have achieved international success. Even so, in an essay on the future of cinema and other visual art forms, John Ellis sees the brightest future for British cinema as independent of the Hollywood tradition.[4]

Whatever the future holds, the days are now over when going to the cinema was a major part of a child's experience. Many of the good things, such as the Saturday morning cinema clubs, have been replaced by television. With many parents owning video recorders, the trip to a Walt Disney film as a birthday or other treat (assuming one can find one showing locally) has been largely replaced by inviting the kids round to watch a hired movie on the video. Issues that used to concern Christians (such as the personal life of film stars, and the effect of one's cinema-going on weaker Christians) are now often irrelevant, or at least pale into insignificance by comparison with the problems of television—which are often very similar.

Yet cinema does have a great influence on children, albeit an occasional, rather than a daily one. To understand this we must consider how we look at films, as opposed to how we look at television.

The nature of film

When we watch television, we are in control of a number of elements in that experience. We can decide how much else is going on in the room. We can decide who else watches with us. We can talk to each other, discuss what we are seeing, or even take time off to do something completely different such as turn up the fire or make a cup of coffee. The images we see are small, contained in a box. We have access to the television controls; we can adjust the volume to what we would like it to be, and we can even distort the image if we want to by fiddling with the controls. We can, above all, turn it off.

We can watch anywhere we like; sprawled on the carpet, or lounging in an armchair, or sitting eating at a table, for instance. We can do other things at the same time; knitting, or peeling potatoes, or polishing shoes, or any one of a number of things that can be done with only an occasional glance. And we can also control the level of light in the room, from darkness to normal lighting levels. For a child watching television, the set is just another item in his family landscape. It is part of everyday life.

When we go to a cinema, everything changes. We leave our homes, the known and familiar furniture and possessions, and we go to a place that is set apart to watch films in. When the projectionist (whom we do not see) decides it is time to begin, the house lights are lowered and the film begins. The other members of the audience are unknown to us. We see images on screen larger than life, faces in close-up magnified to vast proportions; and the wall of the cinema disappears and becomes an opening onto a world created by the film-maker. Television can never do this, for it is too small.

The film sound track in cinemas is sophisticated, multi-

channel, and loud. There are no distractions; it is too dark to
see anything except the film, and many films today have no
interval. We sit in seats that are barely comfortable. Our
very posture dictates that we should look straight at the
screen and nowhere else. Where with television we are controlling the experience, in the cinema the experience is very
definitely controlling us.[5]

It is this difference which makes the cinema ideal for at
least two types of visual communication: horror and fantasy.
The size of the image works in their favour. Science fiction
benefits too. In *2001: A Space Odyssey* the long space ship
moved across an enormous screen, but even the screen could
not contain the whole ship at once. On television the point
would have gone for nothing; in television scale, many objects that are not particularly big have to have the camera
panned across them. But a child who sees *2001* makes the
instant and unambiguous deduction: if the ship couldn't even
fit on to a screen as big as *that,* then how enormous it must
be!

Similarly in *Star Wars* the depths of space are believably
portrayed; in *Close Encounters of the Third Kind* the size
and 'otherness' of the alien ship was illustrated both by the
size of the screen image and the intensity of the light on the
screen;[6] and in *ET* the poignancy of the alien's plight was
emphasized by the fact that he was *not* enormous.

This comparison illustrates the biggest difference between
television and cinema in a child's experience; because television is a familiar object in most homes, its images and
experiences are manageable.

Television's danger, as we have already seen, lies in the
fact that harmful sounds and images can damage a child
either because they are unobtrusive and build up an effect
gradually, or because the child experiences them in a situation—for example late at night—when his normal 'defences'
are down.

At such times, in fact, he is approaching the cinema experience, because what cinema achieves is a direct assault on the viewer's responses in an environment designed to make that impact as powerful—and the viewer as responsive—as can be.

So the power of the cinema is great; when a film makes a statement or presents a fantasy it does so with far more power than television can hope to achieve, and it does so with the viewer at his most receptive.

The child and the cinema

In the case of television, one of the most important tasks of the parent is to make sure that the child does not see material which is designed for an adult audience. But in the case of the cinema it is a simpler matter.

The current system of film classification (administered by the British Board of Film Classification, which also classifies pre-recorded videos) has two categories of film which children under fifteen may see; 'U' (unrestricted) films are open to all ages, and 'PG' (parental guidance) films are open to under-fifteen-year-olds if accompanied by an adult. Consequently, for a child, the problem of seeing material designed for older viewers does not exist. He is not allowed into the cinema in the first place.

Nevertheless, this leaves several matters in which a parent must still take care. With an increasing number of quite recent films being shown on television, a young child who stays up late can see several films a week at home that he would not be able to see in a cinema. There is also the problem of video—a '15' or '18' rated film may be available in the home if the parents have hired it from a video library. And there is of course the possibility that a young teenager will be allowed into a cinema because he pretends to be older than he actually is.

Though these are probably not situations that are likely to happen often, if at all, in many families (because the parents bring their children up not to tell lies about their age, and they make sure that any adult videos are kept out of harm's way), there is still a problem that remains.

And that is the fact that many films rated 'U' or 'PG' contain explicit or implicit material that a parent might well consider to be disturbing.

The risk of confusion

The 'PG' categorization encompasses some films which seem strange entertainment for under-fifteens. It would be an unusually mature fourteen-year-old, for example, who understood much of what is going on in *Careful He Might Hear You,* which is a very thought-provoking Australian film about a little boy being fought over by two aunts. As the film proceeds the characters are developed brilliantly, resulting in a complex and poignant tangle of emotions.

It isn't a film with a strong sexual content, and most of what there is would pass over the heads of young children watching. It has little violence as such, though one of the interesting things about the film is the way that nature is presented as a threat, and there are several frightening storm scenes. Also some episodes of school bullying and domestic quarrelling would probably distress quite a few children.

I would recommend *Careful He Might Hear You* to adults, as a finely crafted, sensitively performed portrayal of a human problem, illuminating the issues it raises with positive understanding. It would not be a great surprise to me to find that Christians had been involved in making it, and in most respects it makes the points about relationships that I myself would want to make if I were directing a film on the subject.

But why would anybody want to take an under-fifteen-year-old child to see it? Conceivably as a rewarding artistic experience—but if so, the risk of confusing the child and introducing fears about the security of his or her own family life is much too strong.

Awarding this film—which I regard as an excellent one—a 'PG' certificate seems to me just to push young children into a confusing world of adult tangles and tensions. Parents who take their children to see it may well have to cope with its after-effects. The classification seems to be unnecessarily broad, and only serves to present parents with a difficult decision.

The risk of distress

Similar decisions have to be made with 'U' films. I went to an afternoon showing of *The Never-Ending Story,* and sat next to a mother with two children, both of whom must have been about eight years old.

The film is a fantasy adventure, which explores some traditional themes which have been stock-in-trade in children's literature for centuries. It tells the story of the search to rescue the land of Fantasia from an advancing evil, and features highly inventive fantasy creatures in a weird and wonderful landscape. It is funny and moving by turns, and though at the end its message becomes rather confused, it is essentially a film that lives in the same kind of world that the Bible talks about; where loyalty, love, courage and faith are all things that are praised.

Like many films of this type, it relies heavily on special effects, and some of the creatures are very impressive; for example there are bizarre dwarves, a luck-dragon, a rock-eater, and a giant bat.

It's here that a parent may have difficulties. The mother sitting next to me in the cinema certainly did. One of the children, at the first appearance of the rock-eater, buried her face in her mother's shoulder and barely emerged for the rest of the film. The other child clung to her mother for reassurance, but watched the film wide-eyed.

I was glad that I had not brought my own daughter, because at one point a horse drowned in a swamp in a scene which was very sad indeed. The episode played an important part in the film, and on balance I think it was justified; but I found it distressing and I am sure my daughter, who is particularly sensitive to such things, would have found it unbearably sad.

The main task of a parent regarding a film like *The Never-Ending Story* is to decide whether it crosses an individual child's threshold of what is frightening or distressing.

This is not the same as whether or not a film is morally acceptable or not; that is a different issue, though the two may well go together. But there are many films with a 'U' certificate which are on the whole positive and wholesome, yet to which some parents will not be able to take their children.

The risk of moral and spiritual harm

Having said all this, there are still some films in the 'PG' classification which present all sorts of problems, and which many parents will be unhappy to think of their children seeing.

An example is the film *Indiana Jones and the Temple of Doom*, which is the immensely popular sequel to *Raiders of the Lost Ark*.

In the great story-telling tradition that includes *Treasure Island, The Thirty-Nine Steps,* and James Bond, *Indiana Jones and the Temple of Doom* tells of a quest set in an Asian jungle, temples and underground caverns. It is superbly filmed, and extremely exciting as the party of Indiana Jones and his two companions pursue the quest. There are some enjoyably hair-raising sequences, such as a banquet in which more and more exotic food is produced, culminating in large insects as the main dish. The Westerners at the banquet react with horror, but good manners compel them to go on eating. Older children will probably find this entertaining.

The film takes a darker twist when the quest goes underground. The first indication that this has happened is the increased level of violence and horror; a sequence shot in a cell with a spiked ceiling that inexorably comes lower and lower, and a sequence in which large and repulsive insects swarm over the floor and drop onto Indiana's woman companion and climb through her hair are both filmed brilliantly and convincingly. There is also an earlier sequence in which the pair wait in their respective bedrooms. The implications of the situation are that each is waiting for the other to make a seduction attempt, wants it, but will not initiate it.

The climax of the film is the discovery of the underground temple. From then on it becomes intensely frightening. The centre of the temple is a pit, out of which crimson flames belch, and into which victims are lowered, thrashing and writhing, strapped to an iron frame, as sacrifices to the evil god to whom the temple is dedicated. During the making of the film, the special effects team devised a robot that could be lowered into the pit to imitate the writhing of the dying victim. The first trial footage was so unnerving and the filmmakers were themselves so disturbed that they arranged more smoke, to cover the worst agonies.

An extended part of the film deals with the celebration of the sacrifice. Afterwards, there's a battle in an underground mine, a hair-raising ride in colliery wagons, and a final dramatic battle on a rope bridge which is one of the most exciting and best-filmed sequences I have seen in cinema.

The effect on the child is very strong, and the sacrifice in the temple is very convincing. In effect the audience are spectators at a celebration of evil. The incantations and the effects are compulsive.

Steven Spielberg, who made the film, has not attempted to minimize its nightmare qualities. He has said that he liked the fact that the film was so frightening. 'It's not called *The Temple of Roses,* it's called *The Temple of Doom*—the warning is clearly marked on the box.'[7]

But is it? With a 'PG' rating, cannot some basic assump-

tions be made about what is or is not likely to be in a film?
No; that is precisely why it has a 'PG' rather than a 'U'
rating.

But how exactly is it supposed that a parent will 'guide'?
Will he or she see the film first, or will they watch it with the
child first time round? And what are the effects of taking a
child out of a cinema during a frightening sequence, thus
removing him from the situation but also depriving him of
the 'happy ending' which might put some of his fears to rest?

These are worrying questions. A film like *Indiana Jones* is
more difficult to make parental decisions about than films
such as the James Bond epics, which have now established a
track record for being awash with violence and promiscuous
sex. At least with such films the parent has some idea of what
the film is going to be like, but there are many 'PG' films
which are very popular with young children and give very
little indication—either by advertising or by their pre-show-
ing trailers—of what they are really like.

The risks to children are the same; a desensitizing of the
child's resistances to the violent and the frightening; an exposure to casual sexual habits at far too early an age; and the
possibility of lasting damage by seeing filmed events and
images which the child is afraid or unwilling to discuss with
his parents afterwards.

Many of the risks of cinema are the same as the risks of
television, but the power of cinema is, as we have already
discussed, much the more powerful of the two. The
experience is channelled directly to the viewer, not diluted
by outside distractions.

Action

How then does a family work out these problems, and avoid
their younger children being exposed to what may be serious
risk? There follow some practical suggestions.

1. Decide what your family's attitude to cinema is going to be

Is it to be a weekly treat, an occasional treat, or a once-a-year treat?

With television a normal part of most homes, the need for cinema is reduced, and with many families suffering from unemployment or a reduced standard of living, it can be an expensive entertainment.

The decision will be affected by where you live. I live in a country village, and there aren't many cinemas locally. In a town, the opportunities will be greater and so will peer group pressure—your children will hear from schoolfriends about films that they have seen, and will want to see them too. If cinema-going is rationed, then it is easier to handle such requests by simply saying that you will add them to the list of films to be considered when the family next goes to the cinema.

When children are older than the age-group we are discussing in this book, such choosing in the past will help them as they plan their own viewing and the demands of peer groups become stronger.

It is possible, of course, to decide that—for your family, at least—the cinema is completely out, that you and your children will never go. It is understandable, in view of the problems raised by so many films, but I would suggest that it is a mistake. Such a decision makes the cinema the problem, not the films. There are enough films like *Chariots of Fire* or *Star Wars* to be able to choose one which your family can see together. Even a once-a-year visit to the cinema is, I think, preferable to the kind of curiosity that builds up when a child has never seen a film in a cinema.

2. Forewarned is fore-armed

Whenever possible, see films before your children do. It is often well worth the investment, if it means that your child can be prevented from accidentally seeing a film which would be the wrong film for him or her to see.

'PG' films should always be previewed if possible. The classifications are allocated by the British Board of Film Classification (the BBFC), who have so far reserved the 'U' category for films which are totally acceptable for all ages. In the opinion of the Board, a 'U' film will cause no problems to any child (though as we have seen, it is not possible to prescribe for each individual child's sensitivities).

The situation with a 'PG' classification is different. The Board's classification is made on the basis that what the film offers, in terms of excitement, enjoyment or other benefits, outweighs the potential harm of certain aspects of the film. So a 'PG' classification is an acknowledgement that the film has passages which may offend or damage younger viewers.[8]

My own viewing of The Never-Ending Story was partly to see whether my daughter would enjoy it; my wife and I had decided that I should see it one afternoon in London. That film is a good illustration of the fact that what I am proposing is not censorship but protection. You are looking at a film in terms of your children seeing it, and you may make decisions which another Christian parent would make quite differently. I decided against my daughter seeing it, but recommended it to other parents whose children would, I believed, enjoy it. They must of course follow the same procedure and give it their own preview first—unless you are able to share out the pre-viewing among a parents' group, when each member can report back to the group about the film. This would be especially useful in a large town with several cinemas, where programmes change frequently.

3. Involve your children in the choice of film

Discuss with them what films they would like to see, and why. Ask them what their friends liked about the films that they have seen. Encourage them to talk about films they have disliked in the past, and why. (This can be linked in with films they might have seen on television.)

The benefits of this are that you will get considerable help in choosing a film which will be enjoyed, and you will be able to recognize and discuss any unhelpful attitudes to films which are developing. At the same time you could share with them some of the results of your pre-viewing. In this way you can prepare your children for films which otherwise they might have problems with.

It is always risky to bundle your family into the car or on to a bus and go to the local cinema to see a film at random—if only because if the child is taken without particularly wanting to see the film, is frightened by it or feels guilty at having seen it, he may well blame you!

4. Talk about the film afterwards

Discuss it as soon as possible, perhaps while having supper. Talk about what you enjoyed in the film. It is very easy to train children into a habit of destructive criticism; but more difficult to train them to enjoy what the film-maker has created, to believe in the imaginative achievements of the film, and at the same time to be aware of the fact that a film is not truth, though it may speak of truth, and that many things are being 'said' in films which do not appear in the script.

It's a matter of setting an example, of showing your children how not to be vegetables staring at a screen, but to enjoy and respond to what is going on.

Discussions like this are not usually easiest at bedtime, and that is one reason why it is good to see films as early in the day as possible. (For several years now I have found it helpful always to go to the afternoon or early evening showing of any film, rather than the late showing; many of the problems we have been considering are just as much problems for adults.)

You should also keep an eye open for any signs that a child has been seriously troubled by a film—unusual behaviour, fear of the dark, sudden questions relating to subjects in the film—and always make time to answer questions fully and talk through any larger problems.

5. *Don't be afraid to complain*

If you are offended by a film, or think its classification is wrong, then take action!

You should act, not only out of concern for your children and other children over the particular film you have seen, but to provide some feedback to those who decide on what films are seen. There has recently been some pressure to extend the boundaries of what is permissible in the 'U' classification, and parents should be especially vigorous in making their views known if the present quality of 'U' films is to be maintained.

So—how do you go about complaining?

(a) Write to the manager of the cinema, stating why you feel as you do. (Don't forget to write also if you are particularly appreciative of a film that has been shown and want to commend the manager for showing it.)

(b) Write to the Local Authority. First telephone your Town or County Hall and ask who is responsible for the local cinemas. Then write to the Chairman of the appropriate committee explaining your criticisms. Take the opportunity to say anything positive you might have to say about local cinemas as well, and be courteous.

Local authorities have varying attitudes to cinemas; not all exercise their powers, preferring to accept the BBFC classifications and leave it at that. But it is always worth while writing.

(c) Write to the local press. This may well be a useful way of alerting other parents, though some newspapers might not print such letters as a matter of policy.

(d) Write to the British Board of Film Classification. You should write to:

The Secretary
British Board of Film Classification
3 Soho Square
London W1.

You may wish to write also to the Chairman, Lord Harwich, at the House of Lords. You should send a copy of your letter to the Secretary. If you decide to send only one letter, address it to the Secretary.

When writing, query the classification, giving as precise details as possible of what it was in the film that concerned you, any local reaction, the results of any other complaints you have made, and any other *relevant* points.

The cinema is one of the most interesting arts of today. British cinema in particular is achieving some remarkable triumphs. As our children grow up there will be much for them to enjoy. But there will be much that will have the potential to harm.

The twin processes of protection and preparation allow children at an early age to see principles of selection and rejection being followed in a family environment. It is here that the foundations for an enjoyment of cinema in later life are laid.

4

Home Computers

I am typing this book at home on a microcomputer. It is running a program called a 'word processor'.

What that means is that the screen becomes my 'typing paper'; I am typing on the keyboard now, and my words appear on the screen as I type. I won't see it on paper until I am happy with what I have written. I can change words round, alter them, try different punctuation, and generally experiment to my heart's content. Then, when I consider it finished, I will type a command and a printer attached to the computer will produce a neatly typed copy.

Word processors are just one example of how computers have, in a few short years, changed the way that we live and work. I estimate, for example, that my computer enables me to produce at least as much work again as I could when I used a manual typewriter. I use less paper; if I decide I need to add a paragraph in the middle of a page I can simply open up a gap in the text and insert it. In the old days I would have had to retype several pages and scrap the previous typed sheets.

But at the same time, this technical marvel dramatically increases my creativity. If, reviewing something I have written, I think it would be improved by deleting a section or adding a section, it is very easy to make the change. Because nothing is on paper until I give the command, I can change the early part of a manuscript as easily as the part I am currently working on. I can instruct the computer, if I wish, to go through my text changing one word for another every time it occurs—an operation that takes only seconds. And the entire book you are holding in your hands was originally stored on a magnetic disk just five inches in diameter.

Cost? Mine is a business machine, with sophisticated facilities. But you would be hard put to find a good second-hand family car for the price at which you could buy this computer today.

Computers for recreation

We currently have two other microcomputers in our home; a BBC, which is used partly for business and partly for recreation; and a Sinclair Spectrum, which was bought to review computer software (computer machinery is known as 'hardware', anything you load into the computer is known as 'software'), and apart from that is used entirely for recreation.

The use of computers for recreation is itself a fairly new development. Output to a screen (often called a 'VDU'—short for Visual Display Unit) rather than to paper, and use of domestic tape recorders as a data storage medium, are both recent innovations. Previously data was stored on large tape reels or on magnetic 'floppy disks'—today, many home micros still use disks as the storage medium.

Today's home computers, with their high-resolution screen graphics and sophisticated sound facilities, have opened up a unique form of entertainment as well as providing facilities for more serious use.

For example, the programs which run on the micros in my home fall into the following categories: games, graphics (art) programs, quizzes, educational programs, filing and indexing systems, accounts software, and several others.

I can connect the computer to the telephone system via an

electronic box called a 'modem', and can thereby contact other computers and send and receive electronic mail. If I wish, I can pay a subscription and have access to the British Library's catalogues by telephone. A device has been invented which will 'read' printed text through an electronic eye and transfer it into the computer. A computer game played over the telephone enables the player to explore a fantasy world in which other players are also exploring—you can talk to them, fight them, or get on with the main task of finding treasure!

It seems the march of progress is endless. New developments and new computers appear every month. And as the technology advances, the prices continue to fall. There are frequent reports that the home computer market is dying, but if that is so it seems to be having remarkably healthy death-throes.

Children and computers

Computers have an instant appeal for children. Affordable, either as presents from adults or by saving pocket money or other income, they also have the fascination of the new technology and arcade games.

Today's young teenagers are particularly adept at computer skills, and many successful programmers are very young. There have been fortunes made (and lost) in what is in some ways like a latter-day gold rush. If you want to sample the strange world of the young computer expert, and the romance that surrounds the subject, read *The Soul of a New Machine* by Tracy Kidder,[1] a true story which describes the race to design a new super-computer.

Though there are many expert young programmers, the majority of children who use a home micro use it mainly as a games machine.

Most of the video games available in the pubs and arcades —such as *Pacman, Galaxian, Defender, Frogger, Donkey*

Kong, and the best-known of all, *Space Invaders*—are available in impressive versions for home micros at a cost that compares very favourably with that of feeding an arcade machine with silver coins.

And video games are just a starting-point—micros are capable of much more sophisticated challenges.

There's an enormous industry associated with micros. To begin with, there are 'peripherals' (things you plug into your computer)—colour screens ('monitors'), sound units, units that give the micro the power of speech, drawing tools, printers to produce 'hard copy', disk drives for easy loading of programs and data, and 'joysticks'—which look much like the name suggests and are used for very accurate control in computer games. There are at least twenty different joysticks for the Spectrum alone. One I have used operates by infra-red signals and doesn't have to be plugged in at all!

Then there are books; handbooks for most popular machines, books about writing your own programs, listings of programs you can type in by hand, and so on; and magazines—my local newsagent carries three magazines for the Spectrum and two for the BBC micro, but there are several more for other machines and a great many in total.

Popular games software retails in a similar way to popular music, with many of the large chains such as W.H. Smith and John Menzies operating a Top Ten weekly chart. The interest value of many games is quite limited; as in pop music there is peer group pressure to be playing the latest games, and there are relatively few long-lasting 'classics'.

As an indication of what is available, the following is a description of some of the major types of games.

Arcade games

These started the craze, and turned children's computing from an egg-head hobby for brainy kids into a recreation as popular as Walkman stereos.

An arcade game is often a shooting game and involves considerable finger-dexterity and a good degree of hand-eye co-ordination.

They typically involve the player in simultaneously shooting at an enemy and avoiding whatever the enemy is shooting back at him. Sometimes avoidance is the whole theme, in that the player has to escape marauding on-screen enemies and negotiate a maze or obstacle course while simultaneously seeking for treasure or other objects.

Success is rewarded by points of various kinds. For example, in *Space Invaders* and its imitators, each hit scored is credited against a total score; and there are bonuses, usually for eliminating an entire battalion of enemies, hitting a specially difficult target, or completing each part of a multi-part game. The player is not only under attack from the enemy but is usually also fighting diminishing resources—a limited number of 'lives', dwindling fuel supplies, increasing difficulties in play as the game proceeds. Where the bonus system includes extra lives, an expert player can play almost indefinitely on some games, and several micro magazines publish lists of high scores, often exceeding one million for games like *Killer Gorilla,* a version of the commercial arcade game *Donkey Kong*.

Some arcade games require patience, nerve, dexterity and a cool hand. One of my favourites, *Snake,* challenges the player to move a snake round the screen, 'eating' coloured dots in his path. Each dot makes the snake grow. As the snake turns corners its tail begins to loop behind it, and if the player moves the snake's head into contact with its body he loses a life. It's great fun . . . and exceptionally addictive.

Strategy games

Many well-loved board games have been transferred to computers. Chess is the obvious example, with programs now capable of challenging grandmasters and giving them a worthwhile game. Other favourites are Othello, Draughts (virtually unbeatable in any computer version), Three-dimensional Noughts and Crosses, Four-in-a-row, and Go.

Backgammon, Blackjack, Patience, and many more are available. A version of Monopoly exists in which one player can challenge five others, all represented by the computer, which plays five separate and challenging strategies.

There have been new games invented specifically for the computer, one of the most intriguing of which is *System 1500*. This is a response to the world-wide concern about young computer experts tapping into security computer systems in banks and government organizations. The game challenges you to break into several imaginary systems, and is reputed to be a stiff challenge even for an experienced 'hacker'.

Logic games are especially suited to the computer. A number of deduction games are available, which, for example, require the player to find the murderer in a detective plot by examining evidence given by the program.

All these computer games develop the same skills in the player as their more conventional board- and card-game equivalents do.

Sports games

Possibly the most bizarre concept in computer games is that of a player sitting alone in front of a micro playing electronic golf. Yet such games are also popular.

Match Point simulates a tennis match, and two players can play or one player can challenge the computer. You can serve, run to the net, change grip, and do many of the things that are possible in an ordinary tennis match. The heads in the crowd swivel from side to side to watch the play, a shadow follows the ball across the court, and if you hit the ball into the net ball boys appear, run across and collect it.

Olympic Decathlon was an older game that spawned many imitators. It challenged the player to 'run' the 1500-metre race by pressing two keys alternately with his second and third fingers, and to participate in several similar 'events'. I can vouch for the fact that it was an exhausting business!

Games simulating football, baseball, motor racing, darts, golf, orienteering and many more are available.

Adventure games

This is a unique type of game which the home computer has made very popular. The earliest, *Adventure,* was written originally for a full-sized computer by two programmers, Crowther and Woods, who are now revered figures in the history of adventure games.

Adventure begins by informing the player that he is standing by a well-house near a spring. What does he want to do?

The player types in a command, and the computer responds. For example, if 'ENTER HOUSE' is commanded, the computer informs you that you are now inside and can see food, water, a lamp and a key. If you then say 'GET LAMP', you are informed that you are now carrying the lamp, and so on.

Any instructions entered will be obeyed, provided they follow a few simple rules of syntax and the situation in the game at that point allows them to be carried out (if you are locked in a prison, for example, the instruction 'SWIM IN THE RIVER' will be rejected by the program).

Eventually you arrive at a grating in the ground. If you did not 'get' the key, you will have to go back for it, because that is the only way to open the grating. Once through, you are in an underground network of caves, tunnels and strange locations. Your purpose: to find treasure and bring it safely out. (There is considerable similarity between such games and fantasy role-playing games, which we will be discussing in our next chapter.)

Some adventure games are now extremely sophisticated, and feature characters that go about their own business in the game, independent of your choices; and there are games in which the player can equip himself with his own choice of weapons and armour beforehand and thereby influence his chances in certain situations.

Graphics are now common in adventure games, so the player can see the landscape he is entering. Some are even animated; *Valhalla,* an extremely innovative game in its time, displayed a scene in which a figure represented the player. Other figures represented characters in the game. If the player did nothing, the other characters simply went on with their own activities, and you saw them on screen giving things to each other, leaving, entering, fighting and so on. At any point the player could join in and affect the course of the story that was unfolding.

This is a field in which innovations are happening all the time. Further developments in computer technology will open up new horizons; for example, video disk technology opens up the possibility of an animated visual adventure, of a quality approaching film; and communications technology makes possible multi-player prospects such as the telephone game mentioned above—its name is 'MUD'(!), short for 'Multi-User Dungeon'.

Educational games

Schools have invested very heavily in computers, helped by government subsidy.

Teachers' reactions to much educational software has been very mixed. Some software attempts to teach simple mathematics but uses methods which are not used in many schools; while some is not presented well for children and does not have helpful interaction between pupil and program. Other educational software is very good indeed and has proved invaluable in the schools.

Educational computing involves specialized peripherals; a 'buggy' (a small robot) might be used to teach the children geometrical and other principles; light-beams, sound-sensors and many other devices all make use of the computer to teach appropriate skills and understanding.

Home micro users can obtain educational games, which range from logic games to simple adventure games. They are of varying quality, and the best way to choose a program to help your child at home is to speak to your child's school computer teacher.

Wargames and other simulations

A further type of game to which the computer is very suited is the 'simulation'—a recreation of a situation incorporating many of the characteristics of the original and allowing the player to change one or more elements and observe the effect on the total situation.

It is very easy for a programmer to write routines to calculate probabilities, given the starting conditions; and one application of this is in a computer wargame. A military unit, let us say, proposes to force-march over mountainous ground carrying heavy machine guns. The computer can quickly calculate the amount of ground that the unit will move each turn—taking into account the weight carried and the rough terrain—and update the map accordingly. War games in which the computer plays one army can be very challenging, as most programs are capable of developing a simple strategy.

A classic computer simulation is *Hammurabi,* in which the player is the ruler of a small ancient kingdom. The program asks the player each year to allocate funds for building, planting and defence; the results of his decisions are fed back into the model and the situation develops each turn. Variants of *Hammurabi* have made the player governor of a space colony, a space trader, ruler of an Italian city-state, and even Prime Minister of Britain.

In the last the player has to make choices from a series of

options—he can cut taxes, build roads, court popularity, etc. The aim is to survive a full term in office.

Some simulations are used in teaching: *Corplan,* a business simulation, is used by some management training schools, and some war simulations are used in military establishments.

How computers can help your child

If you have a micro in your home there are a number of different ways in which you can expect your children to benefit.

Computer literacy

A major advantage of computers in the home is that they demystify the whole technology. Children who will grow up into a world full of keyboards and VDUs can become familiar with such concepts at an early age.

Many parents buy computers for their children in the hopes that at a time of escalating unemployment they will find prosperous careers as programmers and computer engineers. This is, sadly, optimistic; not all children use their home micros to acquire a working knowledge of programming or computer science. But even those who only play games on them are gaining an ease with micro technology which will help them in later life.

Stimulated play

Computers have screens like televisions and keyboards like typewriters; but unlike either, they are two-way. They talk back. It's delightful to see the expression on a child's face, having been asked to type in a name at the beginning of a session, when the computer from then on displays knowledgeable messages such as 'Well done, Eleanor!', or 'What is the correct answer, Lauren?'

A child very rapidly credits a micro with a personality;

losing a computer game can result in the same frustrated response from the child to the machine that has 'beaten' it as would be given to a human opponent. A young child finds it extremely difficult to grasp the idea that the micro is programmed to respond to particular errors in predetermined ways.

Because of this, educational games—once the initial strangeness has worn off—receive great concentration from most children, because instead of talking to a schoolbook they are talking to a tireless 'human' partner.

Patricia Marks Greenfield has written on this subject at length in *Mind and Media: The Effects of Television, Computers and Video Games* (1984).[2]

Enhanced creativity

Even children who do not write their own programs often tinker with existing ones or play with the facilities of the computer.

The music feature on the BBC computer used in many UK schools allows three-part harmony and percussion; besides creating musical sounds via the keyboard, many children enjoy using one of several music programs which turn the computer into a simple synthesizer. Some incorporate very sophisticated graphics which permit music to be 'written' on the screen, played over the built-in loudspeaker, and finally printed out in a permanent copy.

Art programs are also popular on most home micros that have medium or high resolution graphics. In my home we have a 'mouse', a box connected to the computer by a cable, fitting neatly into the hand, and housing a steel ball which enables it to trundle around the desk.

A program written for the mouse turns the screen into a sheet of 'paper', and as the mouse moves on the desk top, corresponding lines and shapes appear on the screen. My daughter enjoys using the mouse enormously.

Programs exist which enable simple designs to be created.

VU-3D for the Spectrum allows the user to design a three-dimensional structure and then draw it on the screen as viewed from different directions and illuminated in various ways.

The repertoire of creative programs is increasing all the time. A child who lacks confidence in drawing, musical performance, or some other creative field, will often persevere with a computer equivalent, because mistakes can be instantly corrected and no teacher is standing near to check on progress.

Personal goals

Computer games offer the incentive of increasing goals at which to aim; higher scores, higher levels of expertise, more and more complex adventures to solve, higher dexterity to negotiate the upper levels of an arcade game.

By contrast television, even at its most creative, does little to extend personal goals. It sets few targets and keeps no measure of progress.

Children are very competitive in playing these games. Magazines such as *Crash!* (for Spectrum owners) are mainly composed of reviews of games and readers' experiences playing them, high scores gained in play, and correspondence about the games.

The simplest games call for merely good hand-eye coordination and finger dexterity. But a clumsy child can teach himself to survive the easier stages and in due course advance. The skills learned at the keyboard may well be reflected in greater manual dexterity in other tasks, and there is a considerable psychological boost for the child in gaining success in a game at which he has had to strive to win.

Problem areas in computers

For a parent, there are many benefits in having computers in the home, as we have seen, but there are also several ways in which they present problems.

The anti-social computer

Computers have been mentioned in one or two divorce actions, and have caused many problems in families where one member, often the husband, becomes obsessively interested in the computer.

The trouble is that a micro is a self-contained box of fun. You can program it to do virtually anything you want, given the necessary peripherals. Those who are interested in programming can often find it difficult to control the amount of time that it takes up—there is always an incentive to spend 'just another half hour' solving a problem. It's a similar attraction that chess sometimes has to serious players.

For children, the appeal of games is very strong, but few games are playable with two players, and those that are are usually played in the one-player mode. The result can be that a child spends hours alone with a computer, and correspondingly less with other members of the family or with friends.

It should be said that the same can be said of any obsessive play. I remember spending hours as a child with my Meccano set, comparatively few of them with other children!

The temptation of lawbreaking

A disturbing aspect of home computers is that a great deal of software piracy goes on.[3]

It is very easy to copy a program; one simply uses the 'backup' facility which is standard on disk systems and is easily arranged on cassette systems. It is even possible, with good-quality tape recorders, to make a straightforward audio copy in the same way that one can copy a music tape from one tape recorder to another.

Because the process is so easy, it is common for one child to buy a game and then give copies to all his computer-owning friends. Various estimates have been made of the extent of the problem, but some software houses have been forced to either reduce their production of cassette software because of it, or stop production entirely.

Recognizing several years ago that there was a piracy problem, the software houses began to devise protection schemes, which today have achieved great sophistication. Unfortunately, many of the more enterprising amateur programmers have taken on breaking the protection schemes as a challenge. There are even copying programs sold, which claim to be able to copy protected software. Though they are sold with a warning that they must only be used for making copies of one's own software for oneself, they are certainly used by many who buy them for making illegal copies.

The position in law is somewhat uncertain, because computer software piracy is a fairly recent development. Nevertheless there have been successful prosecutions, and almost all software is now sold with a stipulation that it must not be copied for resale, lending or gift.

Recent legislation and court cases have not done much to clarify the present confusion in the industry. But piracy is theft, and calling it piracy or treating it as a programming challenge does not make it anything else; yet it remains a fact that many children have tapes containing several dozen illegally copied games and other programs; school computer clubs are often the venue for extended copying sessions; and in the eyes of the law those doing these things are offenders.

Another kind of juvenile computer-assisted lawbreaking received considerable publicity in the film *Wargames;* this is the use of a computer, a modem (such as is described at the beginning of this chapter) and the telephone, to obtain access to another, private computer, usually by working out access codes to unlisted telephone numbers.

Large-scale fraud has been successfully carried out in this way, but young people tend to be more attracted to the activity itself than the profits that can be made from it. They have caused a good deal of inconvenience and sometimes serious damage, but few 'hackers' as they are called are intending to commit fraud. A very successful book, *The Hacker's Handbook,* makes the following disclaimer:

> The interesting thing as far as hackers are concerned is that it is the difficulty of the exercise that motivates us, rather than the prospect of instant wealth. It is also the flavour of naughty, but not outright, illegality.[4]

But elsewhere in the same book the author concedes,

> The sport of hacking itself may involve breach of aspects of the law, notably theft of electricity, theft of computer time and unlicensed usage of copyright material; every hacker must decide individually each instance as it arises.[5]

It's true that most hackers are over fifteen years old, but the computer press is full of hacking news and the subject is endlessly discussed among computer enthusiasts of all ages.

It may well also be true that, like a great deal of software piracy, the primary challenge is in breaking the code. But that doesn't make it legal, any more than breaking a shop window is made legal by not removing the goods.

The curious ambiguity of hacking was well expressed in the comment of an American high school student hacker:

> We knew we weren't doing anything harmful, but we realized we were doing something wrong.[6]

But this is glamorizing something which is basically wrong. The police do not take such a rosy view of the matter. From time to time arrests have been made. In July 1985 seven children were arrested in New Jersey, USA, charged with theft, computer fraud and conspiracy;[7] it was alleged that they had used their home computers to gain access to the computer of a major government contractor, obtained secret military information, and ordered expensive electronic equipment. It was rumoured that they had even succeeded in altering the orbits of US satellites. Though that may sound far-fetched, one thing that hacking has brought to light is the astonishing lack of security given to highly important data-files by major corporations and other bodies. Most pass-words, for example, if reports of hackers are to be believed, are entirely predictable.

Adventure games

The problem of the effect of violence in video and computer games has been much discussed, but a more dangerous prob-lem (because more insidious), is, I believe, the influence of some adventure games.

These games create a self-contained world. The challenge is to understand the logic of that world, to make sense of the things you find in it, and to complete a task that the pro-grammer has set you. The worlds of computer games are becoming increasingly complex, and some are works of art in their own right.

The games resemble fantasy role-playing games very strongly, and as we shall be looking at those in the next chapter, the main points do not need to be made here. But it is worth saying that the themes of many games are similar to those of many fantasy role-playing games, and that they therefore share some of the same problems. In addition they have the extra dimension of solo play against an unseen and usually very clever 'opponent' (usually the programmer who set up the challenges in the first place).

Many of them are fine creations that will enrich your child, but some are not. Parents concerned to ensure that their children's computer hobby is not taking them into troubled waters should keep an eye on the games that are being played.

A related problem is that a few software manufacturers have been extremely irresponsible in marketing soft-porno-graphic software, advertising in magazines that children read. These are usually adventure games, though one entrepreneur produced a high-resolution strip poker game and another a sex quiz programme, neither of which seem to be particularly restricted in their sales.

One manufacturer, Silver Fox, advertised itself as 'the UK's only specialist *adult* software distributor' and in 1983 took a whole page in the popular *Personal Computer World,* advertising such titles as *Soho Adventure, Philly Flasher, Beat 'Em and Eat 'Em,* and *Sex Hunt.* I wrote to the editor and suggested that the advertisement was incompatible with the strong emphasis on children's computing in the magazine. Other readers also complained. The magazine reacted promptly, cancelled the advertisement, and, I would guess, gained a few new subscribers by taking that stand.

Action

For parents who are concerned to make sure that their children's interest in computing doesn't cause problems, the following suggestions may be helpful, as may those in the following chapters on fantasy, which is an increasingly strong element in the hobby.

1. Resist buying a monitor!

This is a separate screen for the computer, and once bought frees it from having to be plugged into the television set. This dramatically increases the opportunities for your child to become a computer recluse, as he or she no longer has to schedule computing hours to fit in with family use of the television or living room. Of course if there is a serious interest it may well be justified, but the decision should be carefully weighed.

Also, don't rush to buy a modem or to allow your under-fifteen-year-old to have one. Even if he or she does not use it to obtain illegal access to private computers, the legitimate use of a modem (accessing public information boards and swapping messages with other hobbyists) can quickly run up a crippling telephone bill.

2. *Forbid copied tapes*

Any cassette that does not have an obviously printed label is probably a pirated copy (though some blank tapes will be needed if the child does any programming). Explain to your child that copying other people's programs is stealing, and use the occasion to encourage selectivity in buying software. The law, incidentally, is particularly vague on the legality of *borrowing* programs, but I can see no problem in borrowing software from a friend and returning it (uncopied) after use, much as can be done with recorded music.

Your child may protest, 'But everyone does it!' To concede that point opens up all sorts of problems when the child grows into an older teenager and has other moral issues to face. Software piracy can be the occasion for some helpful guidelines to your children on morals in general.

3. *Take an interest*

If you don't know how to use the computer, sit down with the instruction book some time and play. Try out some of the games. Glance through the computer magazines. Get a feel for the hobby.

Many children develop their computer interests quite outside the interest and understanding of their parents, who are pleased that their child is playing with the expensive and educational toy that has been purchased and assume that it is the electronic equivalent of extra homework.

This is sad from the point of view of family relationships— that something that is important to the child should be totally incomprehensible to the parents—but it can be dangerous too, as your child may be acquiring attitudes and interests which will not be helpful in the long run.

In Chapter 8 I will be giving some recommendations for computer software purchases which will hopefully give you and your child some shared interest.

5

Fantasy Role-Playing Games

Fighting 'Monsters' underground: wargame group in cave probe . . .
Front page caption in the *Chislehurst Times,* 18 July 1985.

This caption introduced a short article. It described attempts by a number of companies to secure the rights to use Chislehurst Caves, a local Kent landmark, as the venue for 'fantasy war games'.

The Caves had been the subject of controversy for some time. A company that had first advertised them as a venue was at the time of the article being investigated by the police for alleged fraud, but applications from hopeful gamers following the advertisements had been arriving at the Cave offices at the rate of forty a day.

Local residents, in the meantime, had objected so strongly to the use of the Caves for fantasy games that planning permission had been refused to an American company which was interested in a similar project.

So—what was the excitement all about?

Fantasy games of this type are 'real-life' equivalents of fantasy books and indoor games. The participants pay for the opportunity to dress up in costume—usually medieval—and enter a prepared environment: in this case, caves; in the north of England a castle has been used for similar games.

In that environment actors disguised as monsters and other foes wait for the participants to do battle with them, using harmless weapons and realistic simulations of blood and gore. The combatants earn points for their successes and penalties for their failures, but for most who take part the enjoyment has little to do with amassing a high score. It is the experience itself that is enjoyable, of living out in a believable situation the exploits and adventures of fantasy heroes.

> The Caves would be ideal for the games [explained a spokesman for the fantasy role-playing magazine, *White Dwarf*]. The dark passages and echoes lend themselves well to the games. You wouldn't know what was round the next corner. It would really get the adrenalin going.[1]

The appearance of such a story in a local newspaper highlights the growing public interest in fantasy role-playing games.

It is an interest that stems from a number of different sources. In part, the live fantasy games derive from other popular pastimes such as medieval banqueting (in which guests pay to dress up in costume and join in organized eating and exuberance), and Civil War wargames (in which participants dress up as Roundheads and Cavaliers, and recreate the great battles of the past).

In fact the latter activity gives pleasure to many hundreds of spectators, and participants have been allowed to march through London in uniform, beating muffled drums, in a moving commemoration of the death of Charles I.

But a much greater contributing factor is the phenomenal growth of interest, over the past few years, in fantasy role-playing games. Where most participants in the live events are late teenagers or older, a significant—and growing—percentage of the indoor version is made up of young children.

'FRP'—a growth industry

In a shop in one of our major cities, stocked with maps of fantastic countries and books of spells and lore, a Dungeon Master is buying Orcs and Wargs for his army. He knows how many sword-strokes it takes to kill a Warg, and he knows how much damage an Orc can inflict.

The fight will take place in the treasure chamber, but not in a real castle or cave. It will be in the rich landscape of the child's own mind, stranger and more exotic than any real place could be.

There will be rich pickings for the victors. The opposing fighters will be a cleric, an elf, two wizards, a thief and a wise woman. It will be important to have enough Orcs! The fifteen-year-old Dungeon Master thoughtfully contemplates the pages of his *Monster Manual*.

The teenager I've just described is an imaginary teenager, but the picture I've painted isn't a fanciful one. Thousands of youngsters each week enter the world of fantasy role-playing games—or 'FRP', as the hobby is often called. The best known of these games is *Dungeons and Dragons*, but there are dozens of others.

The shop could be in London, Bristol, Glasgow, Liverpool, Aldershot, Cardiff, Manchester—or indeed in any of the towns and cities where games shops can be found specializing in fantasy games.

In such shops you will find detailed maps of fantasy lands, floor-plans of dungeons, buildings and whole villages, beautifully made miniature figures used to represent characters in the games, and hundreds of books ranging from 'scenarios' (ready-made adventures carefully created in an imaginary world) to volumes of weapons, monsters, spells, potions and armour.

It's a fast-growing hobby, appealing to all ages from ten years old upwards, and a fast-growing industry. Even back in 1982 the sales in America were estimated at 150 million dollars.[2] The British magazine *White Dwarf,* which is devoted entirely to the hobby, announced its circulation in June 1985 as nearly 50,000—and its popularity as increasing by 10% per month.

What are fantasy role-playing games?

For anyone used to conventional games, opening a role-playing game box can be quite perplexing. There is no board as such, often there are no counters, and the only items common to almost all games of this type are one or more dice and one or more substantial books of rules.

A role-playing game needs nothing but the players' imaginations and the rule system. Everything else is decoration. *Dungeons and Dragons,* for example, has an enormous supporting industry of manuals, playing aids, miniature figures, plans, charts, maps and much more, but it is still just possible to play it with pencil and paper and no other equipment except the rule book. In fact the 'Basic Set' ('You can start playing right away,' the box promises) contains just two booklets and a set of die, together with a wax crayon to mark the die and some advertisements for other products.

The game is played by a group of three or more people, one of whom is the 'Dungeon Master'. He is the only one who knows what will happen in the game; using either his own imagination and some basic reference books or a published 'scenario' from one of a number of sources, he has planned an adventure and placed it in an imaginary world, into which the other players will come and explore.

The adventure often takes place in an underground dungeon or cave system, and the game-world is usually loosely based on medieval England, though games can be also set in imaginary towns and villages, the Wild West, orbiting space stations, distant galaxies—in any location, in fact, where an inventive designer can imagine a gamable scenario. The historical period, similarly, might be in the past, the present or the future.

Each player apart from the Dungeon Master will first have rolled die to determine the characters he or she will play in the game and the physical, mental and other qualities of that character. Fighters, magicians, clerics, thieves, dwarves—or, in less conventional scenarios, aliens, outlaws, lawmen, space pilots . . . there are many different character types to choose from.

Having decided what character he or she will play, further die rolls determine for the player what armour and weaponry that character will have, and what money or other possessions will be taken into the game.

The majority of fantasy role-playing games follow the same pattern. They are 'fantasy' games, because they take place in the world of imagination; they are 'role-playing' games, because the players are encouraged to enter into the spirit of the game and the characters they are playing.

The object of the game depends on the particular scenario being played. A common theme is the defeat of evil, either in the shape of monsters or individuals. Some scenarios offer the prospects of tremendous wealth, gained by finding treasure in situations of great danger. Others are built round quests, in which the players' characters seek glory.

What is won in one adventure—fame, wealth, magic objects, experience—can usually be taken into the next. The character develops from game to game; in *Dungeons and Dragons* there are several 'levels' through which it is possible to rise, with greater powers attainable the higher one rises.

In the course of the game, dangers will be encountered and obstacles met. The characters will often have to collaborate, sharing their skills and powers with each other in order to do what none could do unaided. There is no 'winner' in the sense that people win more conventional games, and a fantasy role-playing game can last for many weeks—or for a single evening.

The debate

Though 'FRP' is a hobby that has been in existence for only twelve years, it has been the centre of argument and controversy for several of those years. Fantasy role-playing games —and *Dungeons and Dragons* in particular—have been in the news for some time.

An American news story in 1979 attracted widespread interest: police searched a network of steam tunnels below Michigan University Campus looking for sixteen-year-old James Egbert who had been missing from home for three weeks. Friends reported that Egbert, a *Dungeons and Dragons* enthusiast, had talked of playing the game 'for real' in the tunnels—not in the supervised, commercially publicized way of the Chislehurst Caves, but as a scary experiment intended to push the fantasy world as far out as possible into the real world.

James Egbert turned up unharmed in Texas, and there was no apparent link between his disappearance and his interest in fantasy games. A year later he committed suicide. Though Press interest in him continued, it was never conclusively proved that the games were a cause of his obviously distressed mental state.[3]

There have been several other instances of fantasy games being cited in evidence concerning suicides and other tragic circumstances, and as a result public interest and concern has increased.

The hobby's own press has been aware of the bad public relations that have sometimes existed between gamers and the general public. In February 1982 the American magazine *Adventure Gaming* sounded a warning against over-enthusiasm among players of a game called *Killer*. This is a 'grown-up' variant of cops-and-robbers, in which role-players have to 'assassinate' each other by using harmless weapons such as flour-bags and water-bombs.

In December, in California, a young man was shot twice by a security policeman while playing . . . one of the many amateur versions of and precursors to *Killer*. . . . I learned of a town in Texas that reportedly banned the sale of [*Killer*]. . . . I can certainly understand the fears of the city fathers, after some lunatics with replica weapons terrorized the shopping mall.

Here at home, in Ohio, I know of perhaps half a dozen minor injuries suffered in the play of this game. Unfortunately, those injured were not solely gamers; a couple were innocent bystanders. . . . I do strongly resent the fact that the actions of the crazies playing this deviant game are beginning to have an adverse effect on the rest of our hobby. . . . If you do get in a jam playing this game, don't tell anyone that you are an adventure gamer, please.[4]

But public concern has not only been expressed about the physical danger of the games. The moral and spiritual implications have aroused considerable controversy also.

However, it would be less than fair to ignore the occasional concern expressed in the FRP Press about the possible harmful effects of full-blooded FRP on the youngsters who make up a significant percentage of the games' following, or the more frequent discussions in the correspondence columns about the morality of play.

Morality, that is, in the sense of the moral frameworks *within* the game—not the somewhat more substantial question of whether it is moral to play the game at all.

That question too has sometimes been taken seriously by the hobby. Several years ago TSR Inc. in America (the manufacturers of *Dungeons and Dragons*) used the pages of their monthly periodical *The Dragon* to invite any members of the clergy who 'possess firsthand knowledge of the game's helpful, positive influence on those who play it' to write to them.

Two clergymen, at least, wrote to TSR, praising the game and claiming that it had great value in developing imaginative and social qualities in youngsters.[5]

They are not alone. I know of several Christians whom I respect who play FRP with groups of Christians and non-Christians. I have also had letters in response to articles I have written, from Christians who see far fewer problems in these games than in many entertainments currently available for the young.

In recent years, however, there has been a crescendo of criticism from Christian organizations and churches. This has ranged from the frankly uninformed and hysterical, to the thoughtful and well-researched.

A Christian in the South of England, for example, who had apparently not looked very closely at *Dungeons and Dragons,* issued a leaflet in 1984 which described it as a board game. Much reference has been made in anti-FRP literature to the game's 'hero', Elric, who is portrayed in the game manuals making a diabolic sign with his hand; but it is not at all clear from the literature whether the critics understand the very technical use of the term 'hero' in TSR's productions.[6] (Whether all children fully understand is of course also open to question.)

On the other hand, a pamphlet issued by the Spiritual Counterfeits Project, written by Stanley Dokupil—himself a games enthusiast and designer—put together a strong case for caution, based on a sympathetic understanding of what the game's designers and players are trying to achieve.

So this is an issue on which Christians are divided. Some think the games harmful, others think them rewarding. Some consider them to be excellent devices for encouraging group dynamics, social interaction, and imagination; others, while readily acknowledging that the games are often superbly constructed, with real beauty, ingenuity, and imaginative creativity of a very high order, are at the same time extremely worried, for reasons which will become clear as we go on.

The case against FRP

I want now to look at several areas of the controversy sur-
rounding FRP, and, writing as a Christian parent and a
games enthusiast, to suggest some ways forward. A good
way of surveying the debate is to examine some of the statements often made about fantasy role-playing games.

1. 'FRP games foster a fascination with the occult.'

The commonest objection to FRP games made by Christians
strongly opposed to them is that they encourage an un-
healthy interest in the occult. It is argued that the constant
references to monsters and the supernaturally evil—coupled
with the games' invitation to fantasize and project oneself
into the game situation—lead players to fill their minds with
images of evil.

The usual response of those who disagree with this is to
simply point out that reading a detective thriller doesn't
make you obsessed with the idea of murdering somebody,
and neither does playing FRP games turn you into an occult-
ist.

But in truth many who play, and most who design, FRP
games really think the question is irrelevant. They believe
that the occult is only imaginary anyway, and that spells,
enchantments and demonic regions have no real existence.
And if that's the case—then obviously it doesn't matter if
you make them the basis of a game.

Both Christians and those who are not Christians need to
think twice at this point.

For the Christian, the Bible's teaching is clear and authori-
tative. The world of the supernatural, it explains, is very
much a reality. From the Bible we learn that many of the
phenomena and trappings of the fantasy games have real
counterparts. Individuals can learn about the occult and
even develop some ability both in communicating with occult
forces and practising occult activities.[7]

The Bible goes further still. Though such things are possible, it warns severely that they should be left alone. The Christian, therefore, has a direct command from God not to make the occult, and the supernaturally evil, matters for entertainment.

Somebody who is not a Christian but who is concerned for children's mental and spiritual welfare might well also be worried by the content of many fantasy games and the literature that has grown up around them.

It is common in games shops to find—for example—books on the Tarot pack (a method of divination by means of cards which features in a good deal of occult literature), black magic, demonology and in some cases soft pornography.

In a London games shop which has now ceased trading, the American adult comic magazine *Heavy Metal* was regularly on display within easy reach of the very young teenagers who were among the customers. It is an explicit, soft-pornography publication. It featured, among other, similar stories, a serial about a twelve-year-old girl who in several episodes was portrayed very explicitly in sexual foreplay with a humanoid robot. The only reason for its presence in the shop was the link between cartoon art and fantasy.

In the games department of a leading London toy store I listened as an assistant gave help to a father and son. The son, who looked about fourteen, was buying a game with his birthday money. The assistant showed them *Call of Cthulhu*. 'It's a game about the mythos,' he said. Father and son looked blank. The assistant tried again. 'You know—things that lived on earth before man,' he added helpfully.

As I left the department the boy was looking at other games, having decided against *Call of Cthulhu*. Had he bought it, he would have acquired in effect two books, one of which is largely occupied with careful descriptions of the places and people to be found in the novels of H. P. Lovecraft, described by his publisher as 'the Grand Master of heart-stopping, supernatural terror'.[8]

Even if the occult *were* non-existent (and the Christian in any case disagrees that it is), parents of many faiths and none are rightly concerned that games which are compulsively attractive to children as well as adults should have popularized or generated so much associated literature that is violent, sexually explicit and horrific.

2. 'Explicit, technical information on the occult is freely available in FRP games.'

'These are not games, so much as handbooks of witchcraft and devil-worship,' argue FRP's critics. 'On the contrary, the games are fiction,' retort the players and designers.

This is one of the commonest of all objections, and has sometimes been argued by both sides with more passion than thought. For example, as a matter of plain fact, much of the material in *Advanced Dungeons and Dragons* (really a separate game, and much more developed than the Basic Set),[9] with its associated manuals of monsters, fiends, gods and demi-gods, is dreamed up by the game's authors, and some is the result of competitions held among players to find the most innovative monster. Such monsters really do not exist and are pure invention.

However, there is a disturbing core of reality in these games which is derived directly from the literature of the occult, witchcraft and other supernatural spheres of reality. To feed their invention, the games designers have obviously scoured the standard works on these subjects and the fiction that surrounds them.

Some games, such as *Call of Cthulhu,* which we will be considering in detail in the next chapter, are based almost entirely on the writings of writers who wrote explicitly about the occult and the supernaturally evil.

Though explicit words of rituals and spells are usually not given, many games educate their players in the workings of the occult and the supernaturally evil. For example, the Basic Set of *Dungeons and Dragons*—advertised as being suitable for ten-year-olds and upwards—is very informative on such subjects as werewolves, the undead, and so on. The profusely illustrated hard-back volumes of *Advanced Dungeons and Dragons* are even more comprehensive. So far as these matters are concerned the child has actually bought a popular encyclopedia of the occult and supernatural.

Parents should think seriously about whether they want their children to nourish their imaginations with this sort of material—especially in the context of play.

To be fair, there is nothing in the rules of *Dungeons and Dragons* to suggest that the proper way to play the game is to fill one's mind with images of evil. Indeed J. Eric Holmes, who was closely involved with Gary Gygax in the development of the game (he edited the first Basic Set rulebook) has referred to 'the author's apparent Christian bias'.[10] Though his reasons are rather tenuous, would that the same could be said of all FRP!

But the problem does not lie in the explicit rules, but in the structure of the game itself.

FRP games are open-ended. Players can usually choose their own victory conditions. The things to aim for in the game are normally determined by the Dungeon Master. So the content of any particular adventure—the number and type of monsters, the amount of occult and other supernatural activity required of the players—is not prescribed by the rule book.

But the game paraphernalia contains many informative manuals and player-aids to assist the player who does want to explore this area. The metal miniature figures available for fantasy game players are predominantly representations of evil monsters. The prewritten scenarios, which are used by most casual players and many who play very regularly, are almost always set in evil and supernatural situations.

This ought not to surprise anybody who knows the Bible. The story of the human race, as unfolded in the Scriptures, is a story of choices consistently made for evil rather than good.

Call it original sin, the curse of Adam or whatever theological name you like; in practical terms the Bible points out the self-evident fact that, left to our own devices, we human beings prefer to occupy ourselves with war rather than peace, tension rather than harmony, dark rather than light, evil rather than good.

And in the world of fantasy games exactly that appears to be happening.

An advertiser in the October 1984 issue of *White Dwarf*, offered the following monster metal miniature figures: ape, ogre, troll, ghoul, skeleton warrior, liche, lizardman with club, naga, gargoyle, wyvern, seven-headed hydra, mounted Lord of Chaos, Knight of Chaos, minotaur, winged fiend, satanic archdeacon, balrog, manticore, and giant slug. Of course the player using these figures will have to do some research to find out what for example a satanic archdeacon is and what his powers are, and the necessary information is readily available from the same supplier.

(I am reminded irresistibly of a similar situation mercilessly parodied in the pages of the American satirical periodical *Mad Magazine* many years ago. Two spoof advertisements were presented side by side. One offered ex-army guns for sale, promising devastating power and killing capability. 'The firing pins have been removed,' said the advertisement, 'and these weapons now conform to government safety requirements.' The next, from the same fictitious supplier, offered: 'Firing pins, suitable for US forces hand weapons, ideal souvenirs. . . .')

In the same issue of *White Dwarf*, guidance was given to Dungeon Masters under the title 'Beyond the final frontier: role-playing after death in fantasy games'. This was a well-researched article which explained the beliefs regarding the afterlife of a number of cultures (Christianity was not included). It then suggested various game 'campaigns' based on this information. 'Ordeal', for example, has the players assuming the roles of souls of the dead undertaking 'an arduous journey to find their rightful abode'. 'Soul debt' is instructive on contracts with the devil; '. . .all those who worship devils or demons (and, at the referee's discretion, evil deities) will have dedicated their lives to these beings . . . and those who are offered as sacrificial victims to these beings will likewise be dedicated to them unless their own deity sees fit to intervene.'

Christian parents should be thoroughly alarmed by the fact that such magazines are freely available in newsagents and toyshops. Many parents who are not Christians will still be appalled that young children are being given this information and encouraged to play games with it.

The exact relationship between commercially produced fantasy and material that exploits supernatural horror, and the private problems that its consumers might experience, is hard to assess. For example, does the current rash of books on the occult—to be found in most High Street bookshops—*reflect* popular interest in the subject or *cause* it?

However, many counsellors of young people have come across youngsters who became involved in occult activities and have experienced psychological or spiritual disturbance as a result. The counsellors have often reported that curiosity, coupled with the fact that material was available to be explored, is the origin of many problems—the commonest being the ouija board and seances, which are usually introduced into groups for fun, but often have effects ranging from vague unspecified panic to something much more disturbing.

3. 'The games represent a new and unwelcome development in children's literature.'

It is often argued that FRP games belong as much to the world of literature as to the world of games. This argument, with which I agree, is reinforced by the fact that you have to be quite literate to work your way through the rulebooks of most games, and many of them require you to do extensive reading in associated literature if you want to be a Dungeon Master.

For example, Iron Crown Enterprises' impressive and hugely successful series of games based on Tolkien's Middle Earth trilogy must surely have increased sales of the books, and not only the novels themselves. Many fantasy stores also stock compendia of Middle Earth, guides to Tolkien's worlds, the *Tolkien Bestiary,* and so on.

But the argument that the games are part of literature and that horror and the supernatural have always been ingredients of children's fiction ignores the *role-playing* element. There is a great deal of difference between *reading* about witches and *meeting* a witch; and the role-player is encouraged to think himself into the situation as much as possible.

We will return to this subject in a later chapter, where we will be discussing fantasy role-playing books.

4. 'FRP games present the very real danger that children playing them will want to explore and practise occult and supernatural experiences.'

This argument is frequently put forward by opponents of FRP. It is usually countered by such arguments as: 'No—in fact quite the opposite is the case; they teach the importance of working together and sharing abilities for the common good, they avoid the aggressive competition and emphasize co-operation, and they consistently portray the triumph of good over evil.'

I have found that Christians who play these games tend to use this latter argument very often. But though it certainly has considerable force, and it is possible to play FRP games with a very heavy emphasis on co-operation, it's debatable whether the theme of 'good versus evil' is still that of much fantasy role-playing gaming.

Firstly, claims to be defending good against evil are sometimes rather weak.

The novelist Dennis Wheatley prefaced his occult and spiritualist novels with a solemn warning against any reader becoming interested in the occult or trying to emulate the activities of the occultists he described. In his novels good is usually the victor over evil in that they generally end with a pitched battle in which good emerges victorious. However, the books continue to sell on the basis of Wheatley's encyclopedic knowledge of the occult and his skill at making these matters realistic and frightening.

This is clear from the fact that in bookshops and libraries they are sold alongside such books as the horror novels of Stephen King, who does not make the moral claims of Wheatley but sells extraordinarily well because nobody can make the flesh creep with horror like King can. As with many games, it's hard to resist the conclusion that 'good versus evil' is simply an excuse to introduce evil in a suitably entertaining and 'legitimate' way.

Of course this is not equally true of all games, and some based on comic strips have very strong moral themes, as do the various modules of the *Middle Earth Role-Playing* game (from Games Workshop) and the now-defunct though still obtainable *The Fantasy Trip: In the Labyrinth* series. Nevertheless, even the excellent *Middle Earth* series has opted for scenarios set in wild and supernaturally populated regions, and the cover art of the main game box is dominated by a drawing of a supernatural entity of quite fearsome size, which means that purchasers get the impression that this is a game predominantly about exciting and alluringly-drawn evil. Presumably this choice of presentation was dictated by marketing pressures.

It has to be admitted that the alternative—a game devised round an out-and-out quest for good with little emphasis on evil except as an obstacle to be overcome—is difficult to design successfully. *Wizards,* Avalon Hill's boardgame in which players strive to ascend the ranks of 'good wizard' apprenticeships while at the same time joining together to defeat evil and save the world, is simply not a very good game; and the American import *The Ungame* (endorsed by Christian family counsellor James Dobson), which challenges players to share their hopes, fears and social consciences with each other, hardly qualifies as a game at all because the element of competition is completely removed.

In this, FRP only bears out the well-known fact of the creative life: it is easier to be negative than positive, more bad writers write tragedies than write comedies, and a vital, attractive portrait of evil is always easier to create than a vital, attractive portrait of good.

Secondly, a glance at the gaming magazines such as *White Dwarf, Imagine,* and *Dragon*—especially the correspondence columns—will show that many players openly prefer to play evil characters, and relish the detail and scope in the games which makes such an emphasis easy.

It's better [said one games player] to be evil. You get more advantages. . . . If for some reason you have the idea in your mind that you no longer trust somebody, if you chop him down from behind, as an evil character there's no penalty for it.[11]

Thirdly, some players are too idealistic in contrasting these games with traditional war games—'It's infinitely better to join forces against evil than to shoot each other in a simulated battle.' This is something which the games' designers and distributors themselves have often repudiated. For example, Lewis Pulsipher:

The 'wargame' style is how D&D is designed to be played, though it doesn't mean you must play it this way. Players don't play against each other, but can still 'win' or 'lose' according to whether they survive and prosper [my italics].[12]

A good deal of violence takes place in the most moderate of average fantasy role-playing games, even if that violence is directed at targets such as vampires and other undesirables.

Whatever its supporters may claim, *Dungeons and Dragons,* like most FRP games, is derived from medieval combat rules, fills many pages of its present rulebooks with combat procedures, and quite simply *is* a wargame, even though most of its human participants are fighting on the same side!

5. *'Children are best exposed to violence early on, because they will have to come to terms with it in later life anyway.'*

I have had pleasure from games all my life, I have read and enjoyed many of the classics of fantasy literature, and as somebody who enjoys games of all descriptions I can see things to admire and enjoy in fantasy role-playing games.

But whenever the debate turns to the desirability of hardening children to the harshnesses of life, any sympathies I might have for FRP designers and distributors vanish immediately.

Human evil is not like mumps and chicken pox. It's not something to be got over early by deliberately exposing children to infection. Protection can, and should, mean preparation. It should mean that parents use the limited, priceless years of childhood and early adolescence to equip their children to live in a world where not many will give them the same consideration. It should mean that the child grows up at its own pace, able to absorb each new experience knowing that parents and family are at hand, until the time comes for the child to enter the world.

This is not at all incompatible with a child attending a secular school and living in a secular world. It simply means that the preparation must start from the beginning.

It is responsibility that I have as a parent, that I share with my wife and in a real sense my church, and I am not prepared to share it with people who write as follows:

> It's deliberately gruesome. You have to blow a hole through that video shell the kids are enclosed in. They are little zombies. They don't know what pain is. They have never seen a friend

taken out in a body bag. They've got to understand that what they do has consequences. The world is sex, it is violence. It's going to destroy most of these kids when they leave TV land.[13]

So writes Dave Hargrave, creator of the *Arduin Grimoire*, a game 'enhancement' which accommodates dismemberments, genitals skewered on spears, and all manner of sexual and physical violence. Other gamers tend to speak of it in awe. Yet it is readily available in the UK, from sources which will not ask the age of your child before selling it to him or her.

Obviously there is something in Hargrave's argument. He writes in the American context, with the knowledge that many children in America are literally addicted to television and with the spectre of Vietnam haunting him.

And yes, some things probably are best encountered young. It is better for a child's first awareness of death, for example, to be in a home environment where parents can discuss and explain.

But the therapeutic intent of the *Grimoire* is made suspect by its commercial success. At the point of its creation there may well have been a sociological purpose behind it. At the point of sale, it merges into the commercial boom which is FRP.

Worse by far than Hargrave, who had a reason for his violence, is the industry that exposes children to gratuitous horror, and capitalizes on the child's curiosity and willingness to be frightened, simply in order to enhance and decorate the product.

The following extracts from some popular games are typical.

The entire body of one of these monsters is covered with a sort of bluish pus. When a victim is struck by a Hound's paw, a gout of this mucoid stuff is smeared over him. This 'pus' is alive and active. . . (*Call of Cthulhu*).[14]

To the player approached, a Succubus will appear to be the most desirable woman he has ever seen . . . and probably the most willing, since 'she' will offer and provide any type of sexual favour he desires. . . . Each act of love will cost the player 10 Life Points, burned up by the strenuous nature of his activities. ('Ascent to Hell', scenario module for *Man, Myth and Magic*).[15]

A wight is an undead spirit living in the body of a dead human or demi-human. It can only be hit by silvered or magical weapons. . . . Zombies are mindless undead humans or demi-humans animated by some evil magic-user or cleric. ('Dungeon Masters Rulebook', *Dungeons and Dragons,* Basic Set).[16]

Plant and/or special part	*Uses and/or powers*
Birch (White Birch)	. . . . . Venereal diseases
Ergot (Rye Smut)	. . . . . Venereal diseases
Juniper Berry	. . . . . Venereal diseases
Sarsaparilla (China Root, Spikenard)	. . . . . Venereal diseases

(Dungeon Masters Guide, Advanced Dungeons and Dragons)[17]

How many parents really feel that young children are best exposed to these things early?

Do you want your children to play at pretending that they know how to cure venereal disease? Or to play knowing that a night of sex with an evil spirit will drain them of energy?

Conclusion

There are real strengths in FRP games, and in many ways they are outstanding examples of imaginative fantasy which will enrich the minds of the children who play them.

But there are also real problems which should make any parent who has not previously examined the games in detail stop and think very hard indeed.

In chapter 7 I want to look at another phenomenon which is currently achieving remarkable financial success—fantasy role-playing books. We will also look briefly at some types of comics that are available in local newsagents.

Then I want to discuss how, individually and together, we can help our children and make representations to those who distribute these games and books.

But first I want to pause to consider *Call of Cthulhu,* as an example of a game which is clearly and unambiguously intended to simulate a world of oppression, evil forces, and terrifying horror for its own sake.

6

Call of Cthulhu

Crawling, clawing, sliming horror, seeping from the night-tipped pen of that Grand Master of heart-stopping supernatural terror —H. P. Lovecraft. Sample a dark universe peopled with gods best forgotten and strange races best left undiscovered. . . . Savour . . . the grave-fresh tang of total fear.

(Back cover blurb, H. P. Lovecraft *Omnibus 2: Dagon and other macabre tales.)*[1]

Call of Cthulhu (distributed by Games Workshop in Britain) is a fantasy role-playing game based chiefly on the works of H. P. Lovecraft. He originated the Cthulhu Mythos, the subject of a series of books based on occult and diabolical knowledge, and other authors expanded his idea.

Lovecraft was an unusually lurid writer, with the ability to arouse in his readers the kind of dread fear that the memory of childhood nightmares provokes.

The full-colour cover of the omnibus volume from which the above quotation is taken features a frightening illustration: a skeletal lizard-like beast crouches on a pile of severed human heads. They are spattered with blood and some stare out of the cover with glazed, dilated eyes. A wide grin splits the creature's leathery face. In its hand it holds a woman's head. Blood streams from the head's nose and mouth and over the clawed hand of the monster.

I bought a copy of this book from the shop where I purchased *Call of Cthulhu*. Several copies were stacked near the game. Young teenagers were browsing at the shelves.

In the game, the players assume the role of 'Investigators'. They are bent on the destruction of the 'horrors, mysteries and secrets of the Cthulhu mythos'.[2]

The historical setting is the America of the 1920s. Play follows the general pattern of role-playing games; the 'Dungeon Master' is called the 'Keeper'. The combat tables include impaling and the use of baseball bats.

A character has a SAN (sanity) rating. His sanity can be decreased by, for example, 'finding a companion horribly and inexplicably mutilated'. Loss of SAN can make a character temporarily insane.

The game includes a 'phobia list' detailing nyctophobia, teratophobia, xenophobia (fear of nightfall, monsters and foreigners respectively) and many more; and a table of 'typical SAN losses', giving figures for characters 'surprised by corpse . . . surprised by horribly mangled corpse . . . see good friend or relative die . . . meet someone you know to be dead . . . witnessing grisly bizarre occurrence (ie gigantic bloody head falls from heavens)' etc.

The rulebook contains an elaborate explanation of the Mythos, its old gods, entities and daemons. Each being's description is supplemented by a quotation from Lovecraft. The monsters are particularly fearsome, and are described in lurid and compelling detail. As the rulebook says: 'Even the merest glimpse of some of the more macabre horrors can send a character into screaming insanity.'

Besides monsters and nameless fears, the rulebook contains many other disturbing elements. In particular its description of Lovecraft's universe reveals that in the game gods are remote beings.

The universe is ruled by beings known only as Elder Gods, Outer Gods, or Other Gods. Only a few of these are known by name; the majority are both blind and idiotic. They are controlled to some extent by their messenger and soul, Nyarlathotep, and are immensely powerful. Azathoth, the daemon sultan and ruler of the cosmos, writhes mindlessly to the piping of a demon flute at the centre of the universe. . . .

The God of the Bible—indeed, any meaningful aspect of Christianity—is totally excluded from this world.

Although *Call of Cthulhu* is claimed to celebrate the defeat of evil, the package advocates and facilitates the exploration of evil. Players are given a reading list of Lovecraft's works and urged to read at least seven of them as basic preparation for play. The box cover unashamedly invites the reader to—

> enter the awesome universe of the Cthulhu Mythos, those dread tales in which magic, science, arcane lore, and dark destinies irrevocably sear the lives of those for whom the bizarre and the curious have unseemly attraction. . . . This complete role-playing game is ready to use and the fast-moving *Call of Cthulhu* rules provide fascinating fun in a world of gothic horror in the true Lovecraft tradition.

The box also states that the game is recommended for ages 'twelve to adult'.

A player leaves the game knowing much more about the occult, about the supernatural and about the dark worlds of H. P. Lovecraft—'the true Lovecraft tradition'.

It is significant that the designer chose to omit from the game the concept of the War in Heaven which is found in the later Mythos: it 'greatly weakens the original horror of the stark and bleak uncaring universe, to which mankind is left, naked and defenceless'. Everything is stripped from the game, in other words, that diminishes the bleakness of the tortured world that Lovecraft created.

The game comes with ready-to-play scenarios, entitled 'The Haunted House', 'The Madman', and 'The Brockford

House'. Appendices include notes on 'The Cultists' Lair', 'The Ceremony' (in which a demonic messenger destroys worshippers randomly), and notes on the notorious legendary occult book, the Necromonicon. The rulebook concludes with a very thorough bibliography of Lovecraft's works.

This compendium of occult and arcane lore is available in many game shops and by mail from several advertisers in the game magazines. No warning of any kind is given on the box, and in many toyshops and specialist game stores the game is displayed, open, where many young children browse.

Call of Cthulhu is immensely popular. It has been awarded the H. G. Wells Award, the Strategists Club Award, and Game Designers' Guild Select Awards. Scenarios appear frequently in the gaming magazines, and metal miniature figures are available.

I have discussed it in some detail because it is representative of a growing trend in fantasy gaming, and one to which children will be increasingly exposed.

When a Dungeons and Dragons enthusiast argues that his character is a good character and that the scenarios in which he plays are parables of the eternal struggle between good and evil, there is some truth in what he says. But it is just as well to remember that he is a member of an enormous and growing hobby, which also includes such creations as *Cthulhu,* which equates the diabolical and the foul with 'fun', and takes its subject matter from nightmares of a Godless world.

It is increasingly difficult to separate the two. The shops do not divide their stocks or put warning signs around certain games. The fantasy magazines include articles on a wide variety of games, from ones based on Lovecraft to ones based on Hollywood cartoon films.

Helping our children to make real choices involves teaching them about much more than games. And it involves commitment of time and energy on our part.

7

Do-It-Yourself Fantasy and Sweetshop Horror

You circle the temple, keeping just out of reach of the blue-flamed dagger. Barraka unsheathes a scimitar with his free hand, cutting the air about your head with its mirror-like steel but drawing no blood.

If you possess a Flask of Holy Water, turn to 283. If you do not possess this Item, turn to 325.[1]

Joe Dever and Gary Chalk, *The Chasm of Doom*

A human figure steps out. Its skin is a dirty-green colour. Its wide eyes stare *at* you, yet *through* you. Its jaw gapes open to reveal a mouth half full of rotten teeth. It wears ragged clothes. And it is advancing towards you! Resolve your fight with this ZOMBIE. . . . If you defeat the zombie, turn to 114.[2]

Steve Jackson, *House of Hell*

On the children's shelves of most High Street bookshops, you will find an increasing number of books like the ones quoted above. They'll be called 'Fighting Fantasy gamebooks', 'Adventure gamebooks', 'Role-playing adventure books', or some similar title.

They will all have very atmospheric covers, with artwork similar to the art in fantasy role-playing games. But they will be most easily recognizable once you open the covers. Instead of telling the story chapter by chapter, in a fantasy game book the text will probably be organized in numbered paragraphs, several to a page. The story doesn't seem to flow logically; but on closer examination, the structure becomes apparent, whereby readers are directed from one paragraph to another by the results of their individual choices.

At first sight they are quite formidable books. Parents who are already struggling to keep up with their children's expertise in the New Maths and computer programming might easily decide that such mysteries are too complicated to investigate, and pay little attention to what their children are reading.

Others will notice the names of the publishers—Arrow, Puffin and other firms with a long tradition of publishing good books for children—and take the view that if publishers of that calibre have backed the books, then there can surely be no problem.

Still others will be pleased to see their children reading something more substantial than comics.

But some parents, glancing through the books themselves, will look with dismay at the illustrations of horrific ghouls, fearsome monsters and bizarre encounters, and will be disturbed by some of the descriptions and the vocabulary that is used. Their doubts may be made worse when they read newspaper reports like the following:

'Devil Worship' Games Attacked from the Pulpit
Children's games books which describe devil worship were denounced from a church pulpit yesterday, after parents told of the effect the books were having on young readers. Nightmares, anxiety and asthma attacks have hit some children caught up in the new craze for reading the Fighting Fantasy adventure books.

(*Daily Express*, 4 March 1985.)

So what is the problem? *Is* there a problem? And if so, what can be done about it?

The first thing to be said is that this is not a new craze. It is a variation on an old theme. The authors of these books have some impressive gifts, but originality is not one of them.

The background

Ever since somebody thought of illustrating text with pictures, writers have been trying to invent new ways of firing their readers' imaginations. For example, Edgar Wallace's classic thriller, *Four Frightened People,* was published with the last chapter omitted; readers were invited to compete in solving the solution. Novelist John Fowles, to make a philosophical point, supplied two endings to his book *The French Lieutenant's Woman.*

Detective stories have been a fertile testing ground for innovative ideas. One common technique is where the author turns aside from the story to tell the reader that all the clues needed to solve the problem have now been provided. Some authors have been much more sophisticated. Many years ago Dennis Wheatley published a series of detective thrillers, inserted into which were real clues—packets of sawdust, a used railway ticket, a single human hair, a spent bullet-shell, and so on.

Recently, new and exciting ideas have been introduced. One is the 'treasure-hunt' device. *Masquerade,* by Kit Williams, was a beautifully illustrated short fable, concealed in which were enough pictorial and written clues to identify the location of a golden hare set with precious stones.

The search lasted for many months and attracted wide publicity. It turned out that Williams had buried the hare in a public park in Bedfordshire, but hare-seekers were reported diving in West Country lakes and tramping the Pennines with large-scale maps.

Williams's next book has caused booksellers and librarians a great deal of head-scratching. Most simply call it *Untitled.* The problem is that the book *has* no title! The challenge is to discover one. The clues, as in the earlier book, are contained in the text and in the exquisite illustrations. The prize is a marquetry box containing a golden bee—both made by Williams (like the hare of *Masquerade*) and very valuable indeed.

Masquerade inspired a flood of imitations. Some of the more interesting were treasure-hunt board games (Meta-gaming of Texas produced *Treasure of the Silver Dragon* and *Unicorn Gold,* with real and valuable treasures to be dis-covered), and treasure-hunt computer games (Automata's *Pimania* sets increasingly complex problems, concealed in which are clues to the location of a golden sundial).[3]

Other new ways of telling a story have included simply presenting the reader with a bundle of documents, from which the story can be pieced together; and at least one novel has been published in loose-leaf form, and the reader is instructed to shuffle it before reading!

Many of these experiments have been produced in limited quantities for a specialized audience. Those that have been hugely popular have been aimed chiefly at an adult audience, though children have also enjoyed books like *Masquerade*.

Aimed directly at children, however, are the fantasy adventure books.

How the books work

The fantasy book is a logical extension of the fantasy role-playing game (though children don't have to have played the games to be able to use the books). The games rely heavily on imagination, and comparatively little on components, so it is a simple matter to turn a game which consists of not much more than a rule book into a conventional paperback.

TSR Hobbies Inc, who produce *Dungeons and Dragons,* have published a series of adventure books called the 'End-less Quest' series (there were fourteen in print in November 1983). These were early experiments, and are among the least complicated and possibly least representative books of this type.

A good example is *Dragon of Doom*[4] which describes a race to prevent an evil magic-user from plunging the world into death and destruction. The narrative is written in the second person singular: the reader becomes the hero. 'You stand before the Council of Nine,' it begins, 'barely able to control your excitement, though it is mingled with fear.'

The story continues for several pages until the first crisis is encountered and the characters have to make decisions. The reader is offered several options as to how the story could proceed, and against each option is a page number. The reader decides what will happen next and turns to the page indicated for the choice that has been made. Then the story continues until the next crisis, and so on.

Two people separately reading *Dragon of Doom* will experience the story in quite different ways. One might make a wrong choice early in the story and end his (story) life there and then; the other might choose correctly at each point and succeed in saving the world! Neither will have explored all the possibilities of the book. In fact the author suggests that you read it several times, trying out different strategies.

This book and its companions in the series resemble some of the simplest scenarios produced by TSR for *Dungeons and Dragons*. Though such scenarios claim to give the individual a taste of what it is like to play the game with a dungeon master and a party of players, in fact they are simple story lines with a few options for variant development and limited combat rules.

More recent adventure books have become very similar to the games from which they derive. Puffin's 'Fighting Fantasy' books use a game system composed by Steve Jackson, a well-known name in board wargaming and fantasy role-playing games. *Fighting Fantasy* (1984)[5] explains how a group of players can use the system and provides a short sample adventure; the series of Fighting Fantasy game books which began in 1982 with the best-selling *Warlock of Firetop Moun-*

tain[6] is designed as a series of solitaire adventures, for a single reader to explore.

The series is of a much higher literary standard than that from TSR. It is also much more sophisticated in its approach. Where in the TSR series there are a limited number of fixed options from which the reader chooses, in the Fighting Fantasy books the reader himself takes an active part in determining how certain events will turn out by rolling die.

It's a very similar system to that used in the fantasy role-playing games themselves, and in fact there is not much difference between reading a Fighting Fantasy book and playing a solitaire scenario in a fantasy role-playing game, though with some of the limitations described above. But in the latest books of this type, the reader is involved in numerous decisions which call for skill and judgement. It's much more than simply enjoying a book—it is a matter of *playing* a book, and arguably much more satisfying than playing a solitaire scenario in FRP.

There are other adventure books from other publishers, for example the 'Lone Wolf' series from Sparrow Books—one of the authors of which is Joe Dever, a former USA *Dungeons and Dragons* champion. These include charts and tables, and extensive notes on how to play. There is also a Lone Wolf club for children to join, a range of miniature metal figures designed for Lone Wolf scenarios, and Lone Wolf computer software. The world of the fantasy book and the fantasy game are here almost identical.

The risk factor

It should be evident from the brief descriptions I have given that fantasy adventure books are a quite remarkable development.

Dungeons and Dragons and many of its contemporaries were originally devised and played by university students; but the books were clearly intended from the outset for young children. The level of writing in most of them is comparable to that of the books in the *Dungeons and Dragons* Basic Set, which is described as being suitable for children from ten years and upwards. In fact in 1985 TSR published *Tower of Midnight Dreams*,[7] the first in a new series, the 'Dungeons and Dragons Cartoon Show Books', which is obviously designed for very young readers and is based on the cartoon series which has been shown on British television.

What the books have achieved is success in an age range where books are normally not enormously popular.

Add to this the fact that they draw heavily on the world of literature and imagination, that they involve children in actually using their minds (as opposed to sitting in front of the television for hours on end), and that there is a strong element of creativity involved, and it's easy to understand why the books have not only been rapturously welcomed by children but have also been approved by many adults and, indeed, by major publishing houses who have added them to their lists.

So why, one might ask, were the books condemned from the pulpit—and given several column inches in a national daily newspaper?

The minister in question was talking about *House of Hell,* the tenth in the Fighting Fantasy series. He had two main criticisms. Firstly, children reading the books were showing symptoms of anxiety and extreme emotional disturbance; secondly, the context of the book included explicit pictorial and verbal descriptions of occult phenomena and satanic rites. 'Anything of the occult is evil,' insisted the minister. 'We want to keep it well away from our children.'

One mother, he claimed, reported that her son had begun having nightmares. Then strange marks had appeared on his body. 'When I looked at what he was reading,' she said, 'there were pictures of voodoo type dolls with pins stuck in them.' She was so alarmed that she burned the books. Another mother, the minister reported, found her ten-year-old son's health deteriorating and his asthma becoming progressively worse.

The book that the children had been reading is a substantial paperback, with a cover illustration depicting an old house in moonlight, surrounded by a gnarled tree and a number of twisted and deformed skulls. A red-eyed horned being with emaciated, clawed hands and long pointed ears is glaring out of the cover towards you. The title lettering is designed to look as though it is dripping with blood. It's a piece of artwork in the tradition of publicity posters for horror movies, though rather better done.

The section of rules that begin the book has a novel twist. 'You start your adventure unarmed, with no provisions or potions; *and* you have to avoid being *frightened to death!*' (This happens when your 'fear score' exceeds a certain figure.)

In a 'Background' section the scene is set. You are driving along a road at night in pouring rain. It seems that you have been misdirected. ('*Damn!*' says the book. 'You curse the white-haired old man who sent you off along this bumpy track. . . .') Suddenly a figure appears in your headlights. You swerve into a ditch. Though you are sure you hit the person there is no sign of a body.

Suddenly afraid, you realize that the figure you hit looked very like the old man who misdirected you. You leap for your car. It won't start. You see a house nearby and start walking. As you approach, you see that it is ancient and derelict. You climb the front steps.

'Tonight,' says the book, 'is going to be a night to remember. . . . *Now turn over.*' The story proper begins on the next page.

The choices begin in the first numbered paragraph. Will you use the door knocker (turn to 357), the bell push (turn to 275), or have a look behind the house (turn to 289)? (The last will enable you to eavesdrop on a conversation which later turns out to be about human sacrifice and visitation by supernatural evil entities.)

One can't easily summarize a book like this, but the following are a few of the episodes which a child reading the book may encounter.

1. You find yourself in a fight with two men. You can either fight to a finish or break off combat by leaping through a mirror (para. 215).

2. You are asked to prove that you are not a devil-worshipper, by making the sign of the cross. This you do (para. 300).

3. You are in a dungeon. Three prisoners are locked in three cells, 'to await some horrendous fate'. Each begs you to release them. 'Nearest to you is a pretty young girl; her face and fair hair are dirty and she is in tears.' You have to decide which, if any, of the three you will talk to (para. 209).

4. You find an old woman lying in a fourposter bed. When you touch her you realize she is dead. While you watch, her eyes flick open. They have no pupils. What will you do (para. 139)?

5. An illustration (opposite para. 264) shows a naked girl stretched out on an altar dripping with blood. Two figures stand over her, wearing robes, goat-masks and hoods. One holds an ornate knife in a clawed hand, ready to strike. While the nudity is fairly discreet (good use is made of a few well-placed bits of robes!) the style of drawing is aggressive and frightening. In para. 264 you are offered the options of trying to escape, rescuing the girl, or watching the sacrifice.

6. (You have chosen the third option.) There is a scream as the knife comes down. The worshippers smear the blood all over themselves. You take advantage of their excitement to escape (para. 314).

There are various ways of ending the story. All except one involve the player being killed or doomed to some unpleasant experience. They include: being locked in one of the cells (see 3 above); being sucked into a bottle for all eternity by an Evil Genie; being killed by a Hell Demon; and being caught observing the human sacrifice.

There's a danger, in briefly summarizing a book in this way, of giving an unbalanced impression of what it contains. But it is fair to say that the extracts above are representative of *House of Hell*. The book is designed to provide a succession of spine-chilling and horrific experiences, in the framework of a quest—which is simply to escape alive.

It's also fair to say that the book is quite representative of Fighting Fantasy books as a series, though the human sacrifice element is not standard. In the first, *The Warlock of Firetop Mountain*, there are vampires, ghouls, trolls, a warlock and many more. Although some of these beings are well-accepted inhabitants of the world of the Grimms' fairy tales and those of Hans Andersen, in the game book the illustrations (and most of the descriptions) take the imagination into a much deeper realm of horror. And most recent books of this type have a similar, or more extreme style and content.

The parent's problem

The fantasy game books are in libraries and bookshops; when your child goes to choose a book with his pocket money he or she might easily come home with a book describing the blood sacrifice of a naked girl, and so far as I know there are no limits at all on who can buy the books.

Worse, stores that specialize in such items often stock other books which have nothing to do with games at all, as we have already seen to be the case with fantasy role-playing games. I have seen books on spiritism and the Tarot cards (a method of divination) placed on nearby shelves, well within the reach of children, under the general title of 'fantasy'.

But the place to start is not in the bookshop at all, but at home. It isn't enough to take action only when a child is seen with an obviously horrific or occult-flavoured book in his hand. The problem begins much further back.

Early in 1984 Prince Charles (himself a children's author) refused to accept a children's book which was presented to him. It was called *Ghastly Games*. It featured a snakes-and-ladders game played on a cartoon of the human intestines, embellished with crude joke labels. Writing shortly after that event in the *Daily Mail*, author Roald Dahl explored some of the ways in which, he argued, children's literature is being used today to promote a message or ride a hobby-horse.

> In my view it is morally wrong to expose children to propaganda, even for apparently worthy causes. Children are fertile soil and the chances are that *any* idea, attitude or philosophy may grow, once planted there. . . . Children have a right to grow up free of propaganda. At least until they are old enough to make their own judgements, without prompting.[8]

Dahl points to books such as *Jenny Lives with Eric and Martin,* published by the Gay Men's Press, where an idealized homosexual domesticity is portrayed, 'obviously . . . meant to condition very young children'.

It could be pointed out that the *Mail* itself, like any newspaper, is not averse to propaganda on its own account; and its children's letters page presumably contains letters that have been specially selected from the postbag according to some sort of criteria. But Roald Dahl is a best-selling children's author—five million copies of *Charlie and the Chocolate Factory* have been sold—and his views on children's books therefore carry some weight.

Dahl argues very strongly that what is happening is an exploitation of the young, in which children are at risk. And when you remember that the adventure game books which we are considering are among current bestsellers, it's obvious that the definition of what constitutes an acceptable children's book has altered radically in the past few years.

I believe that this is something brought about by the publishers themselves. Most of the fantasy adventure books exploit children's inherent fascination with the supernatural and the strange—think, for example, of the role of magic, witches and wizardry in traditional children's stories—and the appeal of a free-form adventure structure which is much more exciting than a normal story book.

The exploitation is not in the fact that stories are scary and that children are kept in suspense, desperate to know how the story ends. That is a traditional and, of itself, unexceptionable characteristic of adventure fiction. The exploitation lies in the way in which more and more elements are added, which draw on the occult and the violent.

The comment made by Steve Jackson in response to criticism of his *House of Hell* is a typical reaction: 'These games books are harmless fantasy.' The assumption made by Mr Jackson, as by many publishers of children's fantasy, is that devil worship, demons from hell, supernatural phenomena and a personal devil have no reality—so they are legitimate material for use in entertainment.

It's the same rationale that horror-writer Stephen King (who writes for adults) offers: that his books provide a service for his readers because they allow them to exorcize the horror that lies in all of us—but which is an illusion.

Stephen King (two of whose books, *Carrie* and *Christine,* have been filmed and most of whose books have become best-sellers) recorded his views about what he was doing in a most interesting essay which formed the Introduction to his collection of short stores, *Night Shift*:

> When you read horror, you don't really believe what you read. You don't believe in vampires, werewolves, trucks that suddenly start up and drive themselves. The horrors that we all do believe

in are of the sort that Dostoyevsky and Albee and MacDonald [three authors he has previously referred to] write about: hate, alienation, growing lovelessly old, tottering out into a hostile world on the unsteady legs of adolescence. . . . The tale of monstrosity and terror is a basket loosely packed with phobias; when the writer passes by, you take one of his imaginary horrors out of the basket and put one of your real ones in—at least for a time.[9]

Whatever the truth of this—and it contains some—there is a difference, which King does not discuss, between an adult analysis of horror-stories and the effect of those horror-stories upon a child who has no analytical apparatus to shield him or her from the imaginative power of the writer.

But it is a common defence of horror. An example of the same attitude, though much less intelligently thought out, is to be found in certain comics that are available today.

Horror comics

The magazine was lying with the *Beano* and the pop magazines in the local newsagents. 'Enter our nightmare world at your peril,' it warned: 'Not for the nervous!' It was *Scream!* magazine's holiday special issue.[10] It was probably in your newsagent as well. In case you missed it(!) a taste of its contents is given below.

The stories have titles like 'Dracula File', 'Fiends and Neighbours', 'Dungeon Victims' and 'Another Smile from the Depths'.

There are cartoon strips about vampires, witches, executions, a giant cat that eats humans, and a live burial—to pick just a few at random!

There's more. Special features include: a quiz to test children's knowledge of horror literature ('What does the word *Nosferatu* mean?'[11]); colour photographs of executions and torture displays at Madame Tussaud's Chamber of Horrors and the London Dungeon; cartoon jokes featuring witches and ghosts; and a drawing competition in which the children's winning entries portray skulls with worms crawling through eyeballs and sightless sockets dripping blood.

Some of the stories have a particularly nasty twist.

In 'The Witch' a young boy is awakened by the sound of a witch flying on a broomstick outside his window shrieking curses (these are given in full and are pretty authentic). He tells his mother next day; she refuses to believe him. At the public library he studies books on witchcraft and discovers that fox's tails ward off witches. The next night he stays awake; when the witch reappears, he waves a foxtail at her. She falls off her broomstick and the boy rushes to his mother's room—where he finds toads, moles and caged rats piled up on the dressing table. As realization slowly dawns, the witch climbs in through the window, clutching her broomstick. It is his mother.

As he screams in horror she points out that he too has probably inherited occult powers. And in the final frames of the story, the boy succeeds in turning his mother into a frog.

New trends

Ghost stories have been popular for many years, and some of the world's best-loved fairy stories are about wicked witches, friendly giants, fearsome ogres and lovable dwarves. Against such a background children through the centuries have learned valuable lessons about the importance of such qualities as loyalty, friendship, kindness, bravery and many others.

So is it just scaremongering to see something deeply worrying in the proliferation of horror fantasy books in high street bookshops, and in the fact that magazines like *Scream!* are freely available today for children to buy? (And a brief glance at a large newsagent's stocks will confirm that *Scream!* isn't an isolated example—though it was one of the most disturbing.)

No. There are differences.

Firstly, the old fairy stories were not often about the occult or about evil for its own sake. True, they were sometimes scary. Some of the tales of the Brothers Grimm, written in a bleaker age than ours, are liable to give sensitive children nightmares. When my daughter was younger she refused to look at the highly respectable *Three Billy Goats Gruff*, after browsing through it and seeing a particularly alarming picture of a troll under a bridge. Even so, horror for its own sake is a very minor theme in traditional children's literature.

It is also worth adding that distress at the contents of a book is not necessarily a reliable indicator of whether or not that book is morally, spiritually or in any other way dangerous. One of my daughters refused to allow me to finish reading Tolkien's *The Hobbit* to her, because she had glanced ahead and seen that a well-loved character, Thorin, died in a later chapter. She was also deeply upset by *Black Beauty* (I was myself, at her age!), and by one of Jack London's animal stories—she cried herself to sleep after reading it.

But that does not mean that there is anything absolutely wrong with those books; it just means that a particular child wasn't ready for them. The things that upset my daughter were things that are genuinely distressing in real life, and in a sense her tears were part of the process we all have to undergo, of coming to terms with the world in which we live. My responsibility as a parent is to make sure that that process takes place at a pace suited to her, not at some theoretical pace that doesn't take her into account at all.

The distress and horror in such books is treated as distressing and horrible. Thorin's death is mourned *as* death, as a parting, worthy of grieving over. Whatever the promise of afterlife and eternal rest, death itself is a grief and a parting in *The Hobbit* and the reader is invited to be sad.

But *Scream!*—for example—is quite a different matter. It positively wallows in death and horror. Brilliant artwork lovingly captures every tortured nuance of fear and torment.

The heavy humour is relentless—a pair of undertakers searching for dead bodies and being fobbed off with a parrot; a witch complaining that her broomstick has failed its M.O.T.; a board game that sends you back ten squares if you land on the space that says 'A monster is lurking in the cellar'.

Another difference is that the traditional stories introduced evil as an intrusion into the 'ordinary' world. It was seen as something wrong, something that had to be resisted, that didn't belong in the world of everyday life.

In *Scream!* and magazines like it, evil is presented as normal. Everywhere you go in the world of this comic, you rub shoulders with the horrific, the frightening, the dead, the occult. Fear and treachery are everyday things here. Occasionally villains get their just deserts, but the punishment is described with enormous enthusiasm, and the point seems to be not that wrongdoing is punished, but that there is a gruesome punishment to be dwelt on and savoured. The same can be said of *House of Hell* and many other books.

One more difference. In the old fairy stories, children related to adults, and especially parents, in predictable ways. Bad or frightening adults were usually explicitly condemned and often the child hero or heroine overcame them and found better adults to look after them.

But in many of today's books and comics, adults are often portrayed generally as frightening and threatening. The example of 'The Witch' that we have already looked at is particularly grisly; the fact that the witch is the boy's mother seems to make all mothers slightly ominous. In 'A Ghastly Tale', a young boy is visiting his aunt and uncle on what is clearly a weekly visit. The three are seen from behind, seated in front of a television set. The boy is complaining sadly to them that they never speak to him but only sit watching television all the time. He decides to go home. As he goes, the reader's viewpoint shifts for the first time and we see that Aunt and Uncle are in fact grinning skeletons, wearing scraps of mouldering clothes, gazing sightlessly at the television which bathes them in its light. They have obviously been dead for a long time.

The *Scream!* holiday special was published by the IPC Group, one of the country's largest magazine consortiums. It wasn't a nasty kept under the counter. You could find it on railway bookstalls and high street shops, all for the price of a couple of ice creams.

Fantasy role-playing books are freely available in bookshops and game shops. They too are priced within pocket-money range, and are marketed in a way that places them in the gift market as well as the hobby market. They are the kind of books which, glanced at briefly, might suggest themselves as ideal birthday and Christmas presents; combining the educational advantages of books with the entertainment value of games.

I do not think that there is much doubt that parents are presented with a problem with these books and with certain comics, not least because they are so freely available.

But what can be done? How can we help our children?

In the next chapter, we will consider some possible courses of action.

8

Action on Fantasy

In this chapter we will consider how to look at the whole subject of fantasy in a positive way. It contains specific recommendations of games and books to purchase, which are selected as least likely to date and most in line with our previous discussions. While I wholeheartedly recommend every product suggested, it is very important that you do not buy solely on the basis of my recommendations but examine beforehand. What suits one child may not suit another.

I have been necessarily selective; there are many other products which have the same qualities.

1. Getting to know the subject

The most important task is to understand what the present fantasy boom is all about. What is the attraction of the games, books and computer programmes for children? Why have several generations of young people financed international multi-million dollar industries selling such unlikely products as wizards and books of dungeon plans?

The first thing that Christian parents in particular must understand is that Christians began it!

The single most influential book in the fantasy industry is J. R. R. Tolkien's *The Lord of the Rings*.[1] The author was a Christian and wrote in that perspective. His epic three-volume tale and its companion, *The Hobbit*,[2] have spawned hundreds of imitations since, some of them quite badly written and others good books in their own right. But all the imitators to some extent reflect Tolkien's original biblical framework (and he himself was writing in a well-established tradition of moral fable), which is why almost all fantasy products, for example, claim to be about the triumph of good over evil.

Less well-known in the industry are the C. S. Lewis books; he was a friend of Tolkien and wrote the Narnia series and a science fiction trilogy. Both are constructed round biblical images and have similar themes to those of Tolkien.

If you have never read any of these books, read Tolkien's *The Hobbit*; and then *The Lion, the Witch and the Wardrobe*,[3] which is the second of Lewis's Narnia stories. Enjoy the story-telling gifts of both authors, and allow yourself to respond to the wonderful worlds which they create. If you are gripped, you will probably want to go on to the rest of the Narnia stories and *The Lord of the Rings*.

The fantasy tradition includes several modern Christian writers. John Houghton's *Hagbane's Doom* and *Gublak's Greed*,[4] are recent and very successful novels; John White's *The Tower of Geburah*[5] and Stephen Lawhead's Dragon King trilogy (*In the Hall of the Dragon King, The Warlords of Nin,* and *The Sword and the Flame*[6]) create a richly fascinating world with a strongly spiritual dimension. Lawhead's science fiction novel *Dream Thief*[7] is also worth reading. Fay Sampson's *Panglur Ban, the White Cat* and *Finnglas of the Horses*[8] are an interesting variation from a Christian publisher.

Besides these, many books by writers not specifically writing as Christians or for a Christian market are rewarding and satisfying; many teach simple spiritual lessons. *The Wind in the Willows, Watership Down*[9] and others develop the theme of animal fantasy; T. H. White's *The Once and Future King* quartet (start with *The Sword in the Stone*) is a wonderful fantasy of the Middle Ages; and so on, and so on.

All the above books are recommended and are easily available. You may find your children already have copies. By the way, all the books I have mentioned are much too good to be restricted to a child readership!

2. Thinking about fantasy

You may find it helpful to read some of the books written about Tolkien and his successors. Some are by Christians, others not. One of the most helpful that I have read, as a study of what Tolkien was attempting to achieve, is Paul Kocher's *Master of Middle Earth*, [10] but it is best to have read some Tolkien first.

If your children play with fantasy games or read the books, talk to them about fantasy. Try to find out why they like it. Are they good reasons or harmful ones? There are many very wholesome attractions in the literature, and the industry reflects them. But you might find your children are attracted to the occult or the violent for their own sake.

Once you know what the needs are that fantasy is satisfying, you can decide whether fantasy is the best way to satisfy them. You may well find it is; C. S. Lewis wrote that fantasy was for him the image of truth that finally satisfied the restless longing he had known since childhood; it pointed him to Christianity.

A. An action programme on games

1. Get to know the industry

Not necessarily in great depth, but enough to have an idea of what is available.

Be open-minded. There are many games which will enrich your children, and to deprive them of all fantasy would be to impoverish their childhood.

Try to see some of the game magazines—any large newsagent will carry a wide range. Look especially at the reviews and advertisements, one of the best ways of rapidly getting an idea of the market.

If at all possible, try some of the games. Several parents might consider buying a number between them and meeting regularly for a few weeks to play them through.

For your own family, the following are specific recommendations. Once again, it is important that they be individually examined with a view to whether your particular children will enjoy them:

a. *The Fellowship of the Ring.*[11] This is an extremely good two- or three-player board game, which is based on Tolkien's book and reflects some of its qualities very accurately. Though relatively expensive (it costs about the same as the best-selling *Trivial Pursuits*), this is an excellent investment for a family that enjoys games.

b. *Middle Earth Role Playing.*[12] A thorough FRP implementation of Tolkien's world, with great detail and accuracy. It should be *carefully* studied before purchase. It contains elements of violence and horror, but I believe these to be consistent with the integrity of Tolkien's world. Nevertheless, examine before buying. Scenarios are available which recreate specific aspects of Middle Earth history and geography. An American FRP game, *Hidden Kingdom,* is the work of a Christian group and is set in Arthurian times. Published by New Rules Inc. of California, it may be available in the UK in 1986—check your local Christian bookshop.

If games were rated like films, *Fellowship of the Ring* and *Hidden Kingdom* should get a 'U' certificate, and *Middle Earth Role Playing* should get a 'PG'.

c. *Wizard's Quest.*[13] An entertaining family board game, with a fantasy theme and simple instructions. Another 'U' game.

d. *The Hobbit.*[14] An adventure game available for several computers; some versions have illustrations to accompany the game. It is one of the all-time best-selling games and is excellent value for money. A good game to play with young children (some of the puzzles are quite hard). I have played it with a seven-year-old. A 'best-buy' if you have a computer that can run it. The more recent sequel from the same publisher, *The Lord of the Rings: Part I,* is more difficult to play but is very worth while investigating.

e. *Lords of Midnight* and *Doomdark's revenge.*[15] Both adventure games, for the 48K Spectrum computer.

These are the games which as a Christian I most admire, though they have no 'Christian message' apart from the standard Tolkien themes of courage, virtue and fellowship. They create a profusely illustrated world which is itself a very beautiful imaginative achievement, and in that world you raise armies and make alliances to defeat evil. Each is an artistic/literary creation of great power which will develop your child's imagination.

f. *Colossal Adventure.*[16] A version of Crowther and Wood's original game, which will run on several computers. It is still challenging and exciting, and the verbal descriptions of the locations you visit are highly visual. Regarded as quite difficult, especially in this version.

g. *Pilgrim's Progress.*[17] An adventure game based on the famous book. It is not comparable to the games mentioned above—it runs excruciatingly slowly—but is very Bible-based; the publishers, Scripture Union, recommend that you have a Bible nearby while playing! If your child is familiar with current games he or she may be a little disparaging about this one, but it is a good family game and offers useful teaching.

The same publishers produce some excellent and entertaining computer Bible quizzes, all for the Spectrum.

h. *Castle Quest.*[18] An example of an arcade game for the BBC computer. More than just a finger-exercise, it calls for some mental effort as well. Rather expensive (about £14 at the time of writing), but provides a good deal of entertainment.

2. Take an interest in your children's play

This does not mean a paranoid monitoring, but a sharing. Know what is in their toy cupboards and on their book-shelves. Look closely at what is given to them as presents by well-meaning friends and relatives.

It may be that an obsession with fantasy is filling a gap which you have created. What plans do you have to help your child's imagination to develop? Have you exposed your children to music, paintings, beautiful countryside, story-telling, dressing-up? Do you encourage them to be creative —or sit them in front of a television?

Take time from your own crowded day and give it to your children. It may well pay great dividends!

3. If you have complaints, write to the toyshops and the manufacturers

Mobilize your neighbours; local shops are sensitive to public opinion. So too are the toy manufacturers; as we have seen, TSR Inc. have gone to considerable efforts to respond to public concern.

Games are big business. Customer relations are important. So write. But make sure that you have a reasonable know-ledge of the game. You may be reacting, otherwise, to some-thing which is condemned very clearly in the game.

I have found that most companies are open to discussion about their products. It is also encouraging to see that shops are taking the matter seriously. In the *John Lewis Partner-ship and Gazette* of 5 January 1985 a Director of Buying responded to queries regarding fantasy games from his col-leagues: 'We take great care over matters of taste because to do otherwise would cause offence to the great majority of our customers.' A similar comment from a spokesman for Beyond Software was: 'In our experience, games of dubious morality simply do not sell.'[19]

B. An action programme on comics

1. Get to know the industry

There is a strong anti-censorship movement in this country. It argues that horror comics (and video nasties) are both significant social documents, which reflect serious and thoughtful arguments about society and its attitudes.[20]

The point is in some ways valid. But it is too expensive a luxury. While the academics are deriving intellectual satisfaction from a gory comic or a video like *I Spit on Your Grave,* children are being harmed.

Satisfy yourself on this point. Look at the local newsagents. Check what your children bring home. Can you describe, right now, the contents of the comics your children read? Do you encourage or discourage particular comics? Do your children know that you care about this?

2. Talk to the newsagent

Be diplomatic. Assume that the shopkeeper does not know what the comics contain (make sure that *you* do). He may well be as taken aback as you are; often comic racks are maintained by suppliers who visit regularly to 'top up' the stock, and the newsagent is not directly involved.

Now that he knows what the comics contain, ask him what he intends to do about it.

3. Write to the publisher

Write a calm letter, saying briefly why you are concerned. The address of the editorial department is usually to be found in the small print on the contents page or on the back page of the comic.

4. Talk to your children

Encourage them to enjoy healthy things in comics. There are many that are good fun and teach clear moral lessons.

Comics such as *Superman* embody a good standard of ethical teaching and a clearly moral behaviour (which is more than can be said, unfortunately, for the film versions).

In England there has been a strong Christian influence in comics, and a cartoonist from *The Beano* has also contributed to at least two Christian periodicals.

Don't retreat into shocked disapproval. Sit down with the child, look through the comic together, and discuss where you are unhappy, and why.

5. *Consider stronger action*

If your newsagent refuses to discuss the matter, consider organizing a local petition or a boycott.

In the 1950s in America, Fredric Wertham was a key figure in a campaign which removed horror comics from shops, forced new legislation and virtually dismantled an industry—and it succeeded largely by local action.[21]

C. Two positive campaign suggestions

The anti-censorship lobby criticizes Wertham for his lack of understanding of the way comics actually work, and the social and psychological subtleties involved. But in truth, the question that demands an answer is this: which is to be preferred—the survival of horror comics as an interesting socio-literary phenomenon; or the protection of children?

The rights of parents and children are very simple in this respect: we demand the right of our children not to be exposed to gratuitous horror, sexual violence, obscenity, and other human evil, before we consider them ready.

If that right is seriously contested by anybody, then their credibility is destroyed for any caring, committed parents.

I propose a two-stage campaign, concentrating on two achievable targets.

1. A system of warning stickers

It should not be difficult to put into operation a system whereby stickers are affixed to potentially harmful products, similar to film classification.

As I was completing this book, I was encouraged to see a press statement that the U.S. National Coalition on Television Guidance is agitating for a classification system for *Dungeons and Dragons.*[22]

I would suggest, for example, that *Call of Cthulhu* should have at least the same classification as would be given to a sexually explicit and violent horror film. I would like to see *Dungeons and Dragons* with a 'PG' rating.

Of course such a system can be easily abused. But it would have two consequences; it would give parents an immediate guide to content, and it would force shops to control access to restricted material.

To bring this about, all channels of action so far discussed would be necessary. In addition, the campaign should be carried to Parliament, by writing to MPs and if necessary lobbying at Westminster.

Concerned community groups could organize many different types of activity to promote such a campaign. Churches could take a lead. Those with access to the press and the media could use that access to bring the issue to as wide a public as possible.

I have talked to many manufacturers and retailers in the writing of this book, and I believe that many of them would welcome a classification scheme such as I am proposing.

2. A sticker of endorsement

Just as a boycott would influence a shopkeeper to reconsider whether or not to stock something, so a sticker encouraging local people to buy there because the shop adhered to certain standards would also be a strong motivation.

This idea has been used successfully in the north of England by Charles Oxley. I would suggest that shops which are making an effort either to avoid stocking goods which are potentially harmful, or to keep such goods away from very young children, might be willing to display some such notice. The notice could be very simple: 'This shop is endorsed by the Anytown and District Family Shopping Association'. Members of the Association, of course, should be encouraged to shop there! And the sticker would be presented on the basis of the fact that the shop had a responsible attitude towards its child customers.

In neither case am I advocating censorship, but control. That is what the industry has lacked for some time now, and it is better reaffirmed positively than negatively. For many reasons I would be worried to see any game outlawed. As parents and citizens, however, we have every right to insist that only those who want the worst horrors should have to see them.

Finally, and most important, prayer is essential. As parents we pray constantly for the children in our care and for our own responsibilities as we try to prepare them for this rough and wonderful world, while at the same time protecting them from it when they are too small and weak to defend themselves.

Pray in groups. Pray about these things in your church fellowship meetings, in mother-and-toddler groups, in Sunday School teachers' meetings—wherever people meet with those who have a concern for the young.

There is a market in fear, feeding on a massive preoccupation with the occult and the supernatural, that is selling to the young as well as to the old.

Fighting it is not just an exercise in child-rearing. It is part of the universal struggle in which we are all engaged.

9

The Unspoken Risk

Sexual Abuse of Children

Fact: three quarters of all cases of sexual attacks on children involve an adult whom the child already knows.

Fact: many instances of child molestation and assault are never reported to parents, let alone to the police. The victim is often too shocked or embarrassed to say what has happened. Because in most cases the attacker is close to the child, blackmail is also often used to keep him or her quiet.

Fact: sexual abuse of children is on the increase. One in ten are at risk. Shocking stories of child abuse are frequently in the media. Accounts of cruelty, neglect, and exploitation of all kinds are also common.[1]

This chapter deals with one of the most heartbreaking risks that our children face today: child sexual abuse. It is on the increase and there are no safe geographical areas or social classes.

As parents, what can we do to protect our children and help to minimize the dangers to others?

The natural reaction of many is to refuse to think very much about the possibility that their child, or the children of friends and neighbours, might be the victim of sexual abuse.

The stories in the newspapers and on television seem to belong to another world, simply because they *are* news stories. News stories don't happen to ordinary people. There's a danger, we fear, of making our children paranoid; and also of distorting their growing understanding of sex by emphasizing the terrible things that might happen. Do we want our children to see their sexuality as a liability?

That's understandable. As the father of two daughters I have every sympathy with those who find it distressing in the extreme to think about this matter. I live in a country village, surrounded by fields and woodlands, and I don't want my children to grow up fearing to leave the main road in case a maniac might be waiting for them.

But if we are to be of any help at all to our children, some knowledge of the facts is essential.

A widespread problem

Child sexual abuse does not only mean an adult having sexual intercourse with a child (as in incest and rape). It includes any exploitation by an adult of somebody under the age of sixteen for the adult's sexual gratification.

The statistics, in so far as there *are* reliable statistics (and there are few), spell out a painful message. The exact number of cases of sexual abuse involving young children is not known. Because many victims do not report the offence, published figures are certainly under-estimates. But surveys have indicated that between one in five and one in ten girls in Britain have been sexually abused in some way by men in positions of trust or authority.[2]

A 1981 study suggested that 13% of victims were under six years old and 27% were aged between six and ten. A rape centre reported that 22% of its victims were under sixteen years old. American studies found that, on average, child molesters assault seventy-three victims before they are caught.[3]

The Department of Health and Social Security's records no longer maintain separate statistics for sexual abuse of children. The NSPCC's Child Abuse Registers, which do, are still in the early stages.[4]

Retrospective surveys, in which adults are canvassed about childhood experiences of sexual assault, are subject to normal statistical margins of error, such as the fact that memory is fallible and incidents change in significance as one gets older (though there is a remarkable consistency between some survey results and the registers maintained by help organizations working with current cases).

But the figures that are published do indicate that there is a significant likelihood that at least one child near to us will sooner or later experience some form of sexual abuse.

Many people believe the scale and nature of the problem to be very different from what it really is.

Fiona Goble has listed six common misconceptions[5] and the facts to correct them.

1. *That child sexual abuse is rare.* It isn't. Estimates *start* at 1,500 children per year in the United Kingdom.
2. *That people who sexually abuse children are usually strangers to them.* Only a minority are—and these tend to get the headlines. The majority are known to the child and are usually male.
3. *That abusers are totally evil and immoral.* Some are, but the majority are people with severe personality problems. This does not mean that they can be allowed to disown their actions.
4. *That abuse equals intercourse.* Actually this is an extreme form of abuse; many cases may involve a range of sexual activities excluding intercourse.
5. *That all victims are girls.* Most are, but about 20% are boys.
6. *That child sexual abuse within families occurs mainly in isolated rural communities.* There is no evidence at all to

support this.

Some alarming patterns become visible as evidence of cases comes to light.

The typical areas of concern that follow are merely the tip of a frightening iceberg. I have chosen them because social workers and others have identified them as significant problem areas in the work that they are doing.

Abuse within the family

This is the single largest area of risk today. Incest and other forms of abuse are handled regularly by police, statutory bodies and help organizations.

It's debatable whether the incidence of offences is actually increasing dramatically, or whether there has always been a high level of risk and only now cases are coming to light. Whichever of the two it is, the evidence is appalling.

An NSPCC Information Sheet of 1984[6] records almost one case per ten thousand children reported annually to NSPCC Child Abuse Registers in 1983. The Society regards this figure as artificially low because of the unfamiliarity of some of the procedures.

Instances of abuse often go unreported for a long time, for several reasons. For example:

1. The child may simply not understand what is happening and assume that it is part of the normal process of growing up.
2. The child may be threatened by the relative concerned who warns of terrible punishment if the child tells anybody what is going on.
3. The child may be afraid that if the offence is reported, the relative concerned will be sent to prison. If the case involves either of the natural parents or a step-parent, the consequence will be the break-up of the family home.
4. The child may have guilt feelings. These will be intensi-

fied if, as is often the case, the child who is abused has lacked affection and parental love and has therefore initially responded to the advances of the abuser.

In such cases the needs of the child are paramount, followed closely by those of the family. The child has a right, having just been sexually and emotionally violated, not to then experience the break-up of his or her family if it can possibly be avoided.

The Institute of Family Therapy in London and the Great Ormond Street Hospital for Sick Children have both been involved in family counselling, and the Great Ormond Street Hospital has conducted sessions in which the incest offender, after release from prison, is reintroduced to the family under the supervision of a trained family counsellor.[7]

Such sessions are harrowing for all concerned, but the benefit, where a gradual reintegration of the family can be achieved, is enormous.

The Paedophile Information Exchange

Sometimes secret abuse of children is dragged suddenly into the public spotlight.

In November 1984 Charles Oxley was a vital prosecution witness in a trial at the Old Bailey in London. For Mr Oxley, Lancashire headmaster and Christian educationalist, it was the climax of his personal crusade against the Paedophile Information Exchange and the end of an extraordinary story.[8]

PIE was an organization which demanded that the age of consent should be abolished and sexual relationships between adults and children be legitimized. 'Paedophilia', according to the Oxford Dictionary, means 'sexual love by an adult for a child'.

Are you disgusted? So was Charles Oxley. When he heard about the organization in 1980 he was horrified. His immediate thought was that it should be stopped. A seasoned campaigner for public morals, he decided to do something about it himself.

What followed has something of the nature of a detective story. Adopting the pose of an interested but cautious enquirer, he wrote to PIE asking for information, and in 1981 joined the organization. His intention was to find out enough about it to be able to present evidence to the police that would ensure its destruction.

He planned his crusade with military precision. First and foremost he made sure that the police were aware of what he was doing. Then he created a false identity for himself. The tall casually-dressed northerner who attended the London meetings of PIE didn't look at all like a headmaster. 'Dave Charlton'—the false name that he adopted—soon became a very useful person to have around. He was a willing dogsbody, and a competent typist. He was soon helping out with secretarial tasks for PIE.

Charlton/Oxley in due course attended meetings of the executive committee where the PIE magazine *Contact* was on the agenda. Throughout his time as a member, he was informing the police of the activities of the society. Extracts from the magazine were presented as evidence at the Old Bailey trial. The sixth issue advocated sexual acts with boys and girls, arguing that the experience would not harm the children concerned.

At the trial two men were charged with committing sexual offences with children and publishing an obscene article. Charles Oxley's evidence was crucial in securing conviction.

While writing this book I asked him about his experiences. 'Weren't you worried,' I asked, 'that you would find yourself up some dark alley with a knife in your back?'

He grinned. 'No. But I was always worried that the Press might get hold of the story before I was ready to make it public. You can imagine the headlines! It wouldn't have looked very good for a respectable headmaster. . . .'

About PIE itself, however, Charles Oxley has nothing

humorous to say.

'I wanted to find out about this organization,' he told the *Daily Mail*,[9] 'because I felt it was despicable and ought to be stopped.'

It is horrifying to think that an organization existed in this country that was campaigning for the freedom to use children for sexual pleasure regardless of their age.

It is exciting and inspiring that people exist who are prepared to take up the fight on behalf of the infants and youngsters who are too weak to defend themselves. The fight continues; a Bill to outlaw paedophilia has yet to be laid before Parliament.

Runaway children

Dickensian London is often used as a barometer of social progress. By measuring present-day conditions against that period when hundreds of thousands of children were treated as slave labour and subjected to abuse of all kinds, one can see that we have moved forwards as a caring society in many ways.

But in one area of social need we are faced with a problem that approaches Dickensian proportions. Gita Sereny, whose book *The Invisible Children*[10] exposed a frightening picture of runaway children forced into crime and prostitution, spent eighteen months interviewing boy and girl prostitutes aged between thirteen and fifteen in Britain, America and West Germany. She became convinced that it is a growing problem. Common factors in the cases she encountered were:

1. Of the sixty-nine children she interviewed in depth, two-thirds came from strict homes where discussion of sex was forbidden. Twelve had been sexually abused by members of their family in childhood.
2. In all cases communications between parents and children

had broken down completely.
3. Boys appear to be more quickly corrupted than girls. (Boy prostitutes ply for trade in certain streets and pubs in London's West End.)
4. Family background in all cases was one of conflict and psychological pressures.

Gita Sereny compares the 'first-aid' and rehabilitation facilities available in America and Europe with British measures and finds the British to be far behind.

> It may be no coincidence that the case histories I gathered here seem more bleak and devoid of hope than any others. 'Do you think anyone cares?' was, justifiably, the bitter question I was to hear time and time again from these young victims. For victims they are: no child in prostitution *wants* to be a prostitute.
>
> To allow men to use them with impunity is outrageous. To ignore them, as if they were invisible, is a scandal. To lose them—any one of them—is a catastrophe.[11]

Dickens could not have created a more moving record than her encounters with children who, despite the squalor of their lives, were still warm and enquiring, with 'a strangely unsullied innocence'.

These children are not only being robbed of their right to grow into maturity with their sexuality intact and unsold. They are being robbed of their right to a childhood.

The unknown victims

Not all types of child abuse receive widespread publicity. It happens in many sectors of society out of the public eye and in circumstances where it is difficult to secure evidence or convictions. One example is the situation of children in certain of the cults and new religions which have arisen in the past few decades.

In the most publicized cult tragedy of recent years, the

notorious Jonestown mass suicide, when 913 members of the Peoples' Church died, 276 of the victims were children and young teenagers. Stories have emerged of appalling child abuse in the community, including sexual humiliation of young girls as a public punishment.

Like some religious extremists in Britain in the nineteenth century, severe physical punishment is often meted out to children in the cults, in an attempt to 'flog the evil out of the child'. This is one of several findings by Margaret Singer, an American psychologist.

She also pointed to the nutritional deficiencies of some cult diets and the effect on growing children; the frequency with which parents handed over the bringing-up of their children to others so that they themselves could work for the cult; inadequate educational facilities; lack of elementary health care and failure to register children's births; and toleration of, and sometimes encouragement of sexual abuse of children.

A group often mentioned in this context is the Family of Love, which used to be called the Children of God. Sexual promiscuity has been tolerated for some time in the cult—initially, girls were encouraged to seduce likely converts off the streets—and recent reports have indicated that adult–child sex is freely encouraged. It is thought that venereal disease is widespread in the cult.

Roger Daly, Director of Community Relations for the American Family Foundation, expressed concern at the plight of children inside the cults which often insulate themselves from the outside world: 'There seems to be very little capacity for cult groups to receive admonishment from people outside.' He pointed out the rivalry that exists for the child's loyalties between its parents and the leaders of the cult.[12]

In England, the organization Deo Gloria Outreach sponsors various Christian rescue and rehabilitation ministries among young people, including many involved in the cults.

A worker associated with Deo Gloria Outreach supplied me with the following list of ways in which he has found that exploitation of children is happening:[13]

1. Deprivation of normal educational opportunities, e.g. preventing familiarity with such disciplines as language, sciences, maths, and other areas of study which are necessary to enable the child to successfully develop its potential intellectually.

2. Restriction or prevention of normal peer-group contact and socialization through play, education, and other childhood activities of the usual sort.

3. Restriction of the development of vocational skills-potential through exploitative guidance and/or employment of children.

4. Use of children in manufacture or other 'cheap labour' by which others profit from forcing children to work long hours for little or no money, under poor conditions. . . .

5. Incest and other sexual 'favours' may be forced on children by those in custody of them.

6. Going a step further, children may be 'passed around' by adults for sexual exploitation.

7. Yet another step is forcing children into prostitution in order to produce income for their 'custodians'.

8. In conjunction with (5) and (6), children may be forced to pose for pornographic photos, videos or films.

9. Children have sometimes been forced to help with various kinds of theft, including muggings, certain kinds of 'con-tricks', burglary, car theft or shoplifting.

10. Children have been used for begging, street vending and other forms of fund-raising that can be based on appeals to sympathy and generosity.

11. Children may be used in drug-trafficking as couriers, look-

outs, messengers, etc.

12. Children have sometimes been controlled, in any of these other things, by getting them 'hooked' on drugs.

13. All forms of mugging.

14. Beatings, sadism, etc. against children.

15. Restriction of exposure to information, contacts, etc, which would allow or encourage the child to think, choose and act for itself. This goes beyond (1) to (3) in that it . . . prevents them from choosing in their own best interests at any time.

This shocking list of abuses—compiled by somebody who is involved in working with children in Britain—is all the more frightening when it is emphasized that the information supplied refers to children *under ten years old*.

Prevailing attitudes

How does it happen that a society which prides itself on compassion and care can also be facing a problem of such proportions?

Children in the arts

One of the disturbing trends in recent years has been the pushing back of the boundaries of sexual explicitness, and the lowering of age restrictions in several crucial areas of restraint.

The sexuality of young girls has been an accepted subject in many public art forms for several years. *Pretty Baby* and *Taxi Driver* are two of the more 'artistic' ones; the sleazier cinemas show endless programmes of soft pornography—the following, taken at random, were showing in London on 1 August 1985: *Porky's Revenge, Desires within Young Girls, Student Games,* and *Emanuelle in America*. All these are known to involve young teenage girls.[14]

The distinction between 'art' and soft pornography in film is not always clear. *Ecstasy,* which was on release reviewed with other general-release films in serious cinema journals, was later shown in a triple bill with *Massage Girls of Bangkok* at a cinema that claims no pretensions to art.

Also accepted are 'art' photography books such as those by David Hamilton, which feature young girls in erotic quasi-natural poses with a strong undercurrent of lesbian innuendo. Hamilton's photography is romantically lit and soft-focused, showing the girls in lush countryside and silk-draped interiors. At least one of his portfolios has been made into a film (*Bilitis*) and put on general release.

In film and television the boundaries of what is considered acceptable are being pushed further and further back. Channel 4's 1985 season of the films of Jean-Luc Godard included *Numéro Deux,* which contained highly explicit portrayal of sexual intercourse, of an ugly and exploitative kind, between adults. In the film, children were filmed asking the parents about sexual intercourse and later commenting between themselves about watching their parents having sex.

Godard himself introduces the film with the question, 'Is it politics—or pornography? Is it pornography—or politics?'

A good question. While frankness on sexual matters and bedroom nudity are not of themselves wrong, what is very disturbing is the coaching and prompting of children in front of a camera crew, on a film set, to conduct a conversation about sex—a conversation which is not of their making and which is being used in the film to serve purposes which have nothing to do with the relationship between parent and child. It is an ugly, damaging film which exploits its young actors.

One might also mention the role of children in video nasties and child pornography, the use of the child-pornography theme as pseudo-social comment in pulp thrillers like Shirley Conran's *Lace* (1982), the increasing sexual content of teenage pop music (e.g. Michael Jackson and Boy George), and the increasing sexual worldly-wisdom of young children in television comedy that we discussed in an earlier chapter.

The end result is a blunting of the natural instinct to protect the innocence of children.

Abortion

To this can be added the subtle eroding of the child's right to be born in the first place, as abortion virtually on demand proliferates and the acceptable reasons for termination of pregnancy increase.

The possibilities for obtaining information about the child while still in the womb have advanced greatly in recent years. This has prompted what in many cases is simply discrimination against the handicapped—denying the unborn baby the right to birth because it is deformed in some way.

Sometimes the argument for aborting is based on humanitarian principles; sometimes the convenience of the family is taken as legitimate grounds for an abortion, because the 1967 Abortion Act established that an abortion is not illegal if there would be a greater risk to the woman's mental and physical health if the pregnancy were to be allowed to go to full term and the baby be born.[15]

It's a flexible criterion. Many abortions are carried out in the genuine conviction that it is in the best interests of the child. But an increasing number are carried out for other reasons such as the desire of the mother to pursue a career or to limit the size of her family.

To make the life of the unborn child subject to such considerations is to devalue children in our society.

Family structure

In Britain today the family is increasingly under threat. The chief casualties are the children.

Seven out of ten divorcing couples have children. . . . One in two girls who marry while teenagers will be divorced by their thirtieth wedding anniversary. . . . By the age of five, 10% of youngsters no longer live with their natural parents. . . . Such statistics are often quoted, and they are certainly alarming.[16] But other statistics, less frequently quoted, add further cause for concern.

One phenomenon that has been mentioned increasingly in reports of sexual abuse has been called the 'stepfather syndrome'. This does not of course mean that families with stepfathers are inevitably prone to trouble.

On the other hand, the NSPCC's findings are that only 44% of sexually abused children placed on the Society's child abuse registers were living with both natural parents when abused; 36·6% were living with their natural mother and a father-substitute.[17]

A typical pattern, as summarized by Charles Oxley, is:

Father leaves home; mother takes up with boyfriend; boyfriend resents the claims of the toddler or baby on the mother, and under the guise of a caring father, severely chastises the child. This often develops into brutal ill-treatment over a long period, sometimes resulting in permanent injury and even death. . . . There have been many cases of sexual ill-treatment also.[18]

Children have been admitted into the subject-matter of fantasy and imaginative eroticism and sexual enjoyment; the value placed on their very life has been diminished; and their well-being has been threatened by the collapse of the security of a family background; is it any wonder therefore that an increasing number of individuals decide to involve children in the real-life gratification of their sexual fantasies?

What can parents do?

Acknowledging this risk ties together what we have been saying throughout the book. First and foremost, as parents and as adults concerned for children, *we are called to a task of protection and preparation*. In shielding our children from the evil that is in the world and the fact that individuals exist who would want to harm them, we have to equip them and, at the same time, recognize the threat and know how to avoid it.

Secondly, *we are called to a campaign of vigilance.* 'Called' is the correct word, because we read that in the Bible Jesus reserves some of his strongest denunciations for those who corrupt the young and exploit them.

> Whoever welcomes a little child like this in my name welcomes me. But if anyone causes one of these little ones who believe in me to sin, it would be better for him to have a large millstone hung around his neck and to be drowned in the depths of the sea (Matthew 18:5–6).

For Jesus, the damaging of a child's innocence is one of the worst possible evils. For us it should be the same. It is a risk we must identify and seek to reduce. And this, as in so many other areas, means hard work and commitment.

Building trust

The best protection against abuse and molestation that a parent can provide for his or her children is to be often with them, not in the sense of policing their every move and fearing to let them develop independence and maturity, but in the sense of sharing their lives with them, being available and approachable, knowing what is important in their lives and what their hopes and fears are.

Only by building trust will it be possible to reduce the number of cases in which an incident has gone unreported because the child was afraid to tell Dad or Mum what has happened.

In a Christian home, the obvious time when such a relationship will be most solidly established is the child's bedtime, when, praying with a parent and reviewing the events of the day in a relaxed way, any problems that are bothering the child will usually come to light. I have found such times to be the ones when my daughter is most ready to talk about problems at school, fears of various kinds, questions about her relationship with God, and all sorts of other issues.

It's a responsibility and a privilege to build up the relationship of trust over the years. What we are working for is the creation of an environment where security and loving relationships are so strong that if anything threatens them the child's instinctive reaction is to tell a parent.

But telling any adult what has happened is still a traumatic experience. In a much publicized case in December 1984 a man with several convictions for child molesting was inadvertently appointed to a job in a children's day nursery. A few weeks later he sexually assaulted a four-year-old girl. The child, giving evidence to the authorities, showed them what had happened, using her Sindy doll and her brother's Action Man.[19]

It must have been extremely upsetting for her to relive the incident for adults whom she did not know. But even greater stresses may be involved.

Because so many cases of child abuse involve members of the child's family, where a medical examination is necessary it is usually carried out by the police surgeon rather than the family GP. Although the child is not taken to a clinical environment or the police station if it can be avoided,[20] this examination—which can include the ordeal of an internal examination—may well add to the trauma and sense of violation.

In such a situation it is vital that a relationship of trust should exist between child and parents, who can then gently prepare him or her for the ordeal of giving evidence or undergoing physical examination.

Setting safeguards

The building of a relationship of trust involves defining boundaries and giving the child elementary training in how to handle situations where those boundaries are challenged.

It is very important to teach children that some situations are so serious that they justify unusual responses. I was in the home of a neighbour a few years ago when a piercing scream came from the garden. Seconds later one of the older children rushed into the room, seized her mother and unceremoniously dragged her out of the house. The mother stopped what she was doing immediately and went with the child.

What had happened was that a rickety gate had fallen on the youngest member of the family, a toddler who had been attempting to climb over it. Fortunately the child was unhurt.

Afterwards, I commented on the speed with which the mother had been summoned. She explained.

'I've taught them that if there is an accident like that, or if they are in serious trouble of any kind, they're to do anything they like to make me come,' she said. 'I don't mind, so long as I know I'm needed. And I've promised them I'll come as fast as I possibly can.'

Similar teaching should be given with respect to dealing with adults. The child should know that it is permissible to refuse a lift in a car, to decline offers of sweets from strangers, to refuse to engage in games with adults which the child finds distressing. The child's natural tendency to stand in awe of strangers, or to be submissive to somebody because they resemble or wear similar clothes to their parents or teachers, has often resulted in situations harmful to the child.

Children's sense of honour and loyalty can also be a problem, as can fear of punishment if they believe that a situation is partly of their own making. Some child abusers have used this fear by threatening to tell parents if the child does not comply with their demands. Parents should make sure that a child understands that it is sometimes right to break a confidence and even a promise, though they should understand that this is for unusual situations.

The handicap of ignorance

Make sure that your child is aware of his or her sexual development, as and when the information is relevant. Many children have suffered sexual abuse because they just do not know elementary facts about their own bodies. Unscrupulous adults have offered 'sex lessons' which have been another form of sexual abuse, and the child has not told parents because they assume that the parent doesn't want to talk about such things.

It is an area where considerable care is needed, because it is desperately important that your child does not become over-worried about either the possibility of abuse or his or her own physical development.

For example, a child in a home environment can wear fewer clothes and behave less formally than outside the home, and it can become a problem as the child grows older. A five-year-old girl playing naked in a paddling pool in the garden is relatively safe; a twelve-year-old doing so is in increasing danger from passers-by and visitors, who may be among the small but significant proportion of the public who have a tendency to abuse.

Explaining this to her is one of the delicate stages of bringing up a child, because you do not wish her to be ashamed of her body and at the same time you do not want to create the possibility that she might be damaged by others.

The important guiding principle is that prevention is far better than cure. It is a good idea to give basic instruction on avoiding the possibility of sexual abuse in the same way— perhaps even at the same time—as such things as road safety and care when near lakes and rivers. This defuses the intensely personal nature of abuse.

A helpful programme that gives numerous examples of how to ensure prevention is given in *Preventing child sexual assault: a practical guide to talking with children,* by Michele Elliott.[21] Though one or two of her recommendations can be criticized, a copy of this book should be on the shelves of every minister's library, and parent groups in the church should know it is there.

Being a good parent and a good neighbour

Besides concern for one's own children, we should have concern for others. This does not mean becoming a watchdog and looking for abuse in every adult-child relationship one knows of. But it does involve accepting responsibility as a citizen, a neighbour, and a follower of Jesus, who considered the welfare of children as a very high priority.

Signs that a child might have been sexually abused, or is being abused regularly, are similar to those for other abuses: sudden changes in behaviour patterns, emotional instability, night disturbances and nightmares, bedwetting and thumb-sucking in children who have grown out of them, evidence of deep-rooted discontent, and anti-social behaviour.

Any child, whether one's own or a neighbour's, with one or more of the above certainly has some sort of problem. If, in addition, there is a sudden revulsion towards adults, unusual displays of affection, or refusal to be alone with a previously trusted relative or friend—then sexual abuse is one of the possible explanations.

A parent discovers offences in one of several ways: either the child tells the parent, or the parent gains the child's confidence and obtains the information, or a relative or trusted adult outside the family acts as a middle-man. However the information comes, it is devastating.

Where the child is a member of your own family, the first priority is to reinforce the relationship of trust which has been threatened by the misbehaviour of an adult.

Your natural response will be one of anger. That is completely understandable. But anger should not be communicated to the child, who will almost certainly interpret it as directed, at least in part, at him or her. If you remain calm the child will be comforted by that fact and will also feel that the situation is not totally out of control—at least one adult can be relied on.

If the child is from another family, there may well be no alternative but to ask outside authorities to investigate as soon as you have evidence that abuse is being committed.

Certainly where either your child or a neighbour's is concerned, the needs of the child, the family situation, and the gravity of the offence all need to be taken into consideration. There are three authorities who can be approached; the police, the local social services, or a general practitioner. It is a legal responsibility of the two last-mentioned to inform the police when cases of child sexual abuse are reported, so informing them is the same as informing the police.

There are several organizations available to help you. The following are a starting point, and can advise you on local organizations.

National Society for the Prevention of Cruelty to Children,
64–74 Saffron Hill, London EC1N 8RS. Telephone 01-242 1626.

(Also check your telephone directory for local branches.)

Royal Scottish Society for the Prevention of Cruelty to Children,

Melville House, 41 Polwarth Terrace, Edinburgh EH11 1NU.

Telephone 031-337 8539/8530.

Samaritans,
Consult your local telephone directory.
(Samaritans is a confidential telephone counselling ministry staffed by trained volunteers.)

We all pray for our children to be kept safe from sexual abuse. But we have a responsibility to teach them adequate safeguards and to maintain adequate safeguards ourselves.

Teaching our children about the presence of such sad possibilities in the world is part of the responsibilities of parenthood. If we fail in this, then we have failed them indeed.

Drug Abuse

A decade ago it would have seemed unnecessary to include a chapter on drug addiction in a book like this, dealing with the under-fifteens. Today it is essential. The death of four-teen-year-old Jason Fitzsimmons in the summer of 1985 from an overdose of heroin and methadone was just one of a number of tragedies that forced the problem of juvenile drug addiction into the national headlines.

Jason, it was revealed, had been addicted to heroin for two years. Subsequently it was reported that his father was also a heroin addict.[1]

The risk to children

In the first seven months of 1985, thirty-five young people under the age of fifteen came to the attention of Merseyside Police drug squad officers. The Chief of the Drug Squad made the following appeal:

> This is not just a police problem. It is society's problem, and parents have as much responsibility as the police. Parents must warn their children of the dangers of drugs. We don't want another terrible death.[2]

In Barking and Dagenham in East London there was a 66%

increase in drug arrests and drug related offences in the first six months of 1985, compared to the same period in 1984. The drugs squad in the borough believe that children as young as twelve years old are buying drugs in local schools. Heroin was believed to be among the drugs available. The drugs squad dealing with the problem is particularly concerned with the threat to children. The Chief Superintendent explained:

> Drugs in this area, particularly heroin, are a growing menace, and it is alarming when you see the results of drug abuse and the crimes it leads to even among the very young. We are talking about ruined lives and ruined families, and the stories we hear are frightening. The youngsters are buying cannabis and amphetamine sulphate which is regarded as the next best thing to heroin.[3]

In Berkshire legal history was made when Berkshire County Council applied for a full care order for a baby girl who was born suffering from heroin and methadone withdrawal symptoms. Her parents both had a history of drug addiction.

Evidence was referred to at the hearing that suggested that the mother knew that she was pregnant and continued to use heroin, switching to methadone, a substitute, at six months. The application for the full case order was made on the grounds that the baby had been ill-treated in the womb, which set a historic precedent.[4]

A national problem

In 1985 public concern over children and drug abuse escalated. In June an all-party Social Services Select Committee called on the government to act immediately. They demanded a £10 million funding for a five-year campaign against hard drug abuse, tougher rules for doctors prescribing hard drugs, the setting up of National Advisory Centres, and a twenty-four-hour 'hot line' for addicts and their families seeking help.[5]

Anxiety was increased when it became apparent that over-stretched resources at the ports were contributing to the problem. Customs officers were finding it almost impossible to stem the flood of drugs coming into the country, and claimed that another 500 officers were needed. It was estimated that since 1979 heroin traffic had increased by 790%. Prime Minister Margaret Thatcher visited the ports and saw the problem for herself, and returned promising help.

Many drugs come from the continent. Reports from Amsterdam indicate that the drugs problem has increased dramatically. Street prices of soft and hard drugs are much lower than in Britain. Soft drugs are ignored by the police, and several clubs in the city advertise marijuana openly on the menu. At the same time, the police have confiscated large quantities of drugs, and have greatly increased the size of their narcotics division.

Yet it is still the case that a British drug addict can get to Amsterdam very cheaply, and once there can maintain his habit far more cheaply than in the United Kingdom. The abundance of cheap drugs in countries like Holland has a spin-off effect on the drugs market in Britain and consequently increases the risk to the young.[6]

The young people's drug addiction situation has become one of our most serious national problems. There are two chief drugs involved: cocaine and heroin.[7]

Cocaine

Cocaine in Europe comes primarily from South America, and is currently coming through in large quantities. It has been feared that London has been chosen as the cocaine capital of the West, and that this will involve gang warfare on a massive scale.[8]

Cocaine received considerable publicity when the film star Stacy Keach was imprisoned in Reading Gaol for nine months in 1984 after being convicted of smuggling the drug into

Britain. He announced at the end of his sentence that he had stopped using the drug, and spoke out strongly against it.[9]

Always a fashionable drug among musicians and other performing artists, cocaine—or 'horse', as it is called—is said to be widespread in the rock music industry, and many stars have publicly spoken against it.[10]

Although a massive problem nationally, with the prospect of major social unrest to come involving competing 'drug barons', the impact of the cocaine threat on the under-fifteens appears—for the moment—to be an indirect one.

Tragically, this cannot be said for heroin.

Heroin

The traditional picture of a heroin addict is somebody whose arms are punctured with scars from previous injections. But an under-fifteen-year-old addict rarely injects.

Part of the problem with younger children is that heroin is sold as something to be smoked or inhaled. So it seems much less harmful. Many youngsters who are addicts have said that they did not think it was addictive if it wasn't injected. A popular way of taking heroin is 'chasing the dragon'. A quantity of the drug is mixed with other substances, placed on tinfoil, and the foil placed over a lit candle. The heroin mixture gives off fumes which are inhaled through a straw. The mixture is usually called 'skag', and street heroin is often called 'smack'.

The flood of heroin into the country is not yet coming under control. In the major cities addiction has been described as having reached epidemic proportions. The cost of maintaining a heroin habit can be £20 per day—though young children are usually sold the drug cheaply to begin with and free 'starter packs' are common. An addict will pay for his habit by petty crime, and by buying in more heroin than he needs for himself and reselling at a profit. The number of small dealers is therefore very large.

Often under-fifteens are given heroin but not told what it

is. It is given names such as 'angel dust', and children are told that it will give them a good feeling. The absence of a hypodermic syringe makes it all the less likely that the child will associate the powder in the screw of paper with the deadly drug he may have heard about.

The parent's role

The question that must be at the forefront of most parents' minds is, 'How likely is *my* child to be affected?'

The answer is almost certainly, 'More likely than you think.'

Recent reports have indicated that the problem is not confined to the large cities and the North of England. It is spread across the country.

Nor does your child necessarily have to associate with older, unscrupulous children to become hooked. The grim fact is that if your child is capable of trying to puff at a cigarette out of curiosity or bravado, he or she is not going to need much more initiative to try an apparently harmless drug which he or she probably barely understands. How sure can we be that our children will always make sensible choices, when the options do not seem to be conspicuously wrong?

Parents cannot afford to be complacent, or to take comfort from past behaviour patterns. The nine to fourteen age range which is currently being infected by heroin peddling is a time in a child's life which is notoriously liable to behavioural change, insecurity, and unpredictable decisions. A child may try heroin, for example, in an attempt to prove his maturity to himself, in much the same way as he might have tried cigarettes.

The bleak fact is that relatively few very young children become regular cigarette smokers after the first experimental puff, whereas the effects of heroin are addictive.

Protecting our children

We must pray especially hard for all children known to us, as the drug situation in Britain today is a desperately serious one. There is little hope of a dramatic improvement, and children will be increasingly at risk. We should pray for ourselves, that we will be able to create the kind of home environment which will minimize the attractions of drugs; and we should pray for our children, that they will be helped and strengthened in situations where temptation is placed before them.

I believe very strongly that if either parent smokes tobacco, they should stop. It is very hard to argue with a child against drugs, if a parent is dependent on nicotine. Much the same can be said of regular and excessive drinking.

Far fewer accidents are caused by the use of cannabis than by the use of alcohol, and soft drugs do not account for a massive proportion of the national mortality statistics in the way that tobacco does. I don't believe that this is a case for legalizing cannabis, and I am sure that the same comparisons cannot be made with heroin, which is a killer in its own right. But a lot of time will be wasted in arguments if cigarette smoking and a nightly 'habit' of three pints in the pub have to be justified before drugs can be criticized.

Create an environment of open discussion in your home regarding drugs. Start the discussion when the children are seven or eight—don't wait until they may be faced with the problem at school. Obtain all the information you can. Leaflets are available from:

> Department of Health and Social Security
> Alexander Fleming House
> Elephant and Castle
> London SE1 6BY

and

> Health Education Council
> 78 New Oxford Street
> London WC1A 1AH.

You should also ask for information from your doctor, the

police, your local library and your local Citizens Advice Bureau, all of which will be relevant to your local situation.

If you live in one of the major drug problem areas such as Liverpool, or the Wirral or London, ask your local Social Services office whether any local self-help groups or parents' action groups exist. You will get a good idea from them as to what the extent of the risk is in your neighbourhood and the schools.

Visit your child's school and find out what provision is made for teaching children at an early stage about the dangers of drugs. If there is inadequate provision, write to the head teacher, and go to parent-teacher association meetings to make the point.

How to tell if a child is using heroin

As with all abuses, any sudden and radical behaviour change should alert parents to the possibility that something is going seriously wrong.[11]

A general withdrawnness from family life; long periods of solitariness; loss of interest in activities and hobbies that have previously been important in the child's life; a lowering of achievement at school; moodiness, frustration, unwillingness to join in family social occasions; and evidence of stealing or other small crimes—these are all warning signs which might point to drug abuse.

Addicts with a 'heavy habit' will show very erratic behaviour, as the time for the next 'fix' approaches. Sometimes physical symptoms will be present at this time, including shivering and the symptoms of 'flu; the eyes of a heroin addict can be dilated and his manner drowsy and over-relaxed.

Should you be in the company of an addict who has just taken the drug, you will see extraordinary euphoria, animated talking, and probably contracted eye-pupils.

How to help

It is initially unthinkable that a child who has been well brought up and who has been loved and cared for, often sacrificially, should ever become a drug addict; but it happens sometimes, just as teenagers can become unmarried parents or break the law under the influence of alcohol. Everybody makes foolish mistakes, and some mistakes are more disastrous than others.

If a child known to you shows any of the symptoms I have described, then make a special effort to spend time talking with him and being available if needed. It would be wise to lock valuables away, and also medicines—he may need money to buy more drugs, and some addicts will steal medicines in the hope that they contain something that will satisfy their needs for a time.

Try to find out if a situation has developed which is making him look for comfort in drugs. Has anything changed in the family? Are important decisions waiting to be made? Has the child recently changed schools? Are there medical problems?

Surely the aim of Christian parenthood is to build a relationship with a child such that even if something so appalling as drug-dependency develops, the child will feel eventually that he can talk to his parents about it.

If, having observed the child and spent time with him, you think that there is a drug problem, go to your doctor and your minister. You need specialist help and spiritual support. Ask your doctor to recommend local organizations which help parents whose children are using drugs. Ask your minister if he knows of any Christian organizations specializing in drug-related problems.

At some point, you will have to ask the child straightforwardly whether he or she is taking drugs.

You may find that you are lied to, and that many lies have been told for some time. Be prepared for this—behaviour is often erratic when drugs have been used. Write down any information that your child gives you about prices, quantities, and where and from whom the drugs were obtained. This information will be helpful to the police in subsequent investigations.

Whatever course of treatment is prescribed, your child will need your total support while it is going on.

If your child isn't taking drugs

If none of the foregoing applies to you, there is still every need for you to become involved with the battle against drugs.

The likelihood is that over the next few years the problem will penetrate more and more parts of Britain and more and more sectors of society. A marquis of twenty-nine and a marchioness's daughter of twenty-eight have both admitted in court to being addicts.[12] From the slums of Toxteth to the splendours of Blenheim Palace, the drug epidemic is making its mark.

What the church must do is to build up an army of informed and compassionate Christians who are aware of the dangers and are willing to do something about it. We should be involved in volunteer organizations, counselling centres, church initiatives, local authority schemes—we should take any opportunity to be involved.

We should campaign for more policing, better control of the drug market, more enlightened treatments; we should agitate for proper resources to be given to those fighting in the front line against drug abuse. Fund-raising and publicity campaigns for voluntary organizations involved might be undertaken. Leaflet distribution and other routine tasks could be carried out to support organizations active in the field.

It is the responsibility of every parent to do *something*. It may be that all we can do is to pray; but that is a vital part of the task. This is potentially the biggest risk our children run; and fighting it will take time, energy and faith.

Conclusion

The drug problem, like all the others we have been considering in this book, calls us back to our twofold task as parents; that of protection, and that of preparation.

It's an awesome task, as we contemplate the numerous problems and complexities of modern life. Even living in a small village, I can see many of the things which I have discussed in this book appearing as potential problems for my children. In a city, the task of parenthood is an even greater challenge. There is so much that young children must be protected from, and the modern city is an environment full of potential harm, into which our children will one day have to go on their own.

The casualties, as the newspapers and media tell us every day, are enormous. Our local government authorities can hardly cope with the victims of exploitation, cruelty and despair. Unemployment, drugs, and a dreary joylessness reach out and touch most young people in Liverpool's Toxteth, for example.

What risks our children run! Many of them have not been mentioned in this book. For example, in Bradford glue-sniffing has become such a major problem that the City Council has appointed a Community Advice Worker for Solvent Abuse.[13] The rise of petty crime is yet another problem that can create peer-group pressure on children. So is juvenile alcoholism. And so on . . . and so on.

Small wonder that we are sometimes tempted to wonder why we ever brought children into a world so full of threats and dangers. It is easy to despair, not least as we read the papers and listen to the news.

And yet there is a great deal to encourage us. I would repeat what I wrote at the beginning of this book; in writing it, I have become convinced that while not since Shaftesbury have so many children been so at risk, at the same time not since Shaftesbury have so many people been fighting for the rights of children, both materially and spiritually.

It is, too, in many ways a wonderful time to be a child. Opportunities for leisure and for education abound. In theory, it doesn't matter what your background is; you can become an Olympic athlete or a professional snooker player, join a professional theatre company, form a rock band, go to college to study Asian history, and so on.

Our role as parents is to prepare children for the world they will live in, while at the same time protecting them from it until they are ready. It means hard work. It takes years of committed parenthood to build a child's confidence and self-image to the point where he or she will be able to handle unemployment, if work is not available. It takes a legacy of many loving hours in family life to equip a child to grow up into a world which has little enough love to spare. It takes weeks and months and years of everyday Christian living to root a child's faith in the practicalities of daily life, and allow that faith to grow into something that will not be shaken when the stresses come.

An impossible challenge?

The Bible doesn't say so. It speaks of children as 'a heritage from the Lord' and 'a reward from him' (Psalms 127:3). Parenthood is a 'crown' (Proverbs 17:6), and is everywhere spoken of as a special trust from God. Nowhere in Scripture does God commiserate with us for having such a burdensome task! Instead, we are told that the task is a reward, a sign of God's love.

It is God's involvement that makes the difference. He knew that our children would be born into our time and not into fourth-century Peru or twenty-first century Albania. We are not here by accident. Our children and we ourselves are in the good plan of God, and so is the world itself, which is why it is worth living in.

Of course, there is a great deal that is wrong with the world. But we are not tackling it alone. God is involved. Jesus prayed for our protection in his last prayer with his disciples: 'My prayer is not that you take them out of the world but that you protect them from the evil one' (John 17:15). He, above all, knew the risk factor.

In our parenting we are undertaking a task that is completed. We have the assurance to let our children go into a world in which God is sovereign. Was it not Jesus himself who told us?

> I have told you these things, so that in me you may have peace. In this world you will have trouble. But take heart! I have overcome the world (John 16:33).

Appendix

The Video Risk

When I began to write this book, media attention was being focused on the problem of 'video nasties'. The campaign against them began in 1982 and came to a crescendo in 1983. The *Daily Mail,* for example, launched its own campaign, and several programmes on television drew attention to the dangers that such films represented to young children who might see them in their own or friends' homes.

Three factors played a major part in the campaign.

(1) The British Videogram Association and the British Board of Film Censors (as it was then) were both involved in formulating a voluntary code of practice, with government approval. Work on this had been proceeding for some time, and the BVA had initiated its own enquiries.

(2) In the summer of 1982, the Parliamentary Group Video Enquiry, under the chairmanship of Lord Nugent, began. Its findings were published, under the title *Video Violence and Children,* in 1983 (Part I) and 1984 (Part II). Part III was published in paperback in 1985.[1]

(3) Also in 1982 Graham Bright, MP for Luton, introduced a Private Member's Bill in Parliament. This, known as the Video Recordings Bill, received the Royal Assent during 1984, and is now law. The progress of the Bill through Parliament was marked by a substantial measure of government support, where previously the government had declared its

intention of waiting for the BVA and BBFC findings to be made available.

Britain has the highest ownership of video cassette recorders in the world, and the figure is growing.[2] The rise in numbers of machine-owners has meant a corresponding rise in commercial video films available, and of libraries distributing them.

A list of video films featured significantly in the campaign. This was the 'DPP's list'. It was a list of films that had been found obscene under the Obscene Publications Act of 1959, or were currently being considered for prosecution by the Director of Public Prosecutions. In September 1983 thirty-two films were listed; by 1984, there were fifty-three. The films on the list constituted for many people the definition of a 'video nasty', though few had ever seen one.[3]

According to the Parliamentary Video Group Enquiry, however, an appalling number of children had seen more than one 'video nasty'—the phrase, incidentally, seems to have been coined by Mrs Mary Whitehouse in 1982. The Enquiry's Reports offered shocking figures which indicated, for example, that 50·7% of all boys under sixteen years old surveyed had seen at least one film on the DPP's list, and 41·7% of all girls under sixteen.

In 1984 Martin Barker edited a book of essays,[4] highly critical of the campaign, and arguing against censorship of 'video nasties'. The arguments included the following charges:

1. The government switch from caution about legislating against video nasties to wholehearted support of the Bright Bill was a politically motivated move and was intended to restore public confidence in the government's commitment to law and order.
2. The Parliamentary Group's statistical methodology was extremely weak, and its findings were highly tendentious. Brian Brown, who had been closely involved with the

academic work of the Reports, repudiated the final publication and accused the Academic Working Party's organizer, Dr Clifford Hill, of wanting a pre-judged result rather than accepting the criticism of various academics involved that the research was inadequate.

3. Several contributors affirmed the value of video nasties as offering an opportunity to exercise the 'dark . . . side of the imagination'.[5] They claimed that the videos provided a sociological document with 'a crude infrastructure of moral justice'.[6]

There is no doubt that the Parliamentary Group's Reports do have some serious problems, being based on a small statistical base and surveying a relatively small period of time. Many of the points made by opponents of the campaign are valid.

But that is not the main point. Many documents produced in the heat of social anger have been less than perfectly researched, and have selected data to prove the argument they want proven. The question that the Reports raise is this: is there a problem, or is there not?

Graham Bright has pointed out that the demand for a Bill came originally not from a Christian lobby but a teaching lobby.[7] There was considerable concern about the evidence that teachers came across in their daily work, of young children being psychologically distressed by seeing obscene and violent video film at home. Often their parents had hired the films and left them lying around at home.

Whether the Reports have got the scale of the problem correct or not, there clearly is a problem, and a large one.

In the Reports, the Group described videos:

The scenes of violence in this film include a skinned rabbit being hung by its rear legs, gutted and dismembered. The carcass is then mutilated and beaten. An electric drill is placed in a man's back. Blood is seen spurting out. He is also drilled in the chest and his body mutilated with the drill. . . (*Driller Killer*).[8]

Later they return to the house to find out if Jennifer is really dead. Seeing the men awakens an animal rage within her and she turns into a creature with only one goal—revenge! She kills each man in a unique, elaborate manner. She makes love to Matthew and then hangs him. She seduces Johnnie in the bathtub and castrates him. The others go out to avenge their friends' murders only to confront Jennifer and come to violent and shocking ends. . . (*I Spit on Your Grave*).[9]

That films such as these are being seen by young children, there is no doubt. If that is so, one has to ask what effect the films have on the youngsters who see them.

Members of the anti-censorship lobby have argued that it is a gross violation of personal liberty to deprive people of the right to have such videos in their homes. They have predicted serious social repercussions from censorship.

There comes a time, however, when liberties have to be traded. The essays edited by Martin Barker make some valid points about what the videos are saying; they argue that many are not destructive, but factual comments on the bleakness and cruelty that characterizes modern life. As a Christian who believes in the historic fall of man, I recognize the point that is being made.

But against the liberty to have video nasties available as a commentary and a social mirror, plus various other justifications that are put forward, must be placed the liberty of the child to grow up at his or her own pace; to mature without having, as a first experience of sexual awareness, a distorted and violent portrayal of sex on a video; to go to sleep at night without images of horror and anger returning unbidden in nightmares.

In a refreshingly common-sense article, Polly Toynbee challenges the anti-censorship lobby:

It is for them to prove that scenes showing the repeated rape and torture of women do not incite more attacks on women. To most people it seems highly improbable that there is no connection whatever between the thought on the screen and the deed on the street.[10]

The effects of video nasties do not have to be proven academically. The burden of proof is on those who want to keep them; in the meantime, to observe the damage, one has only to look at a child who is exposed to violence on any visual medium. The child changes.

There is no adequate way of ensuring that video nasties will not continue, if unchecked, to fall into the hands of an increasing number of children; and of the two liberties, I think most of us would want to trade our rights as adults for the right of the child to have a childhood.

For that reason I am encouraged that the Bright Act is beginning to bite, and the DPP's list is now almost of historic curiosity, owing to draconian fines that the Act imposes.

However, a problem remains. As video recorders increase, there will be an increasing number of 15- and 18-rated videos in homes, and there is a growing chance that any child might see one—in a friend's house if not their own.

Our agenda for action must therefore be the same as it has been throughout the book.

1. Protect the child within the home, by keeping any 15- or 18-rated materials, which we might (even quite legitimately) have in the house, locked securely away or put completely out of reach.
2. Prepare the child for a time when he or she will have to make his or her own choices. Share the reasons why you make the choices you do.
3. Discuss the problem of videos of all kinds with your friends and fellow parents.
4. Talk to local retailers and video libraries. Ask them to keep the violent and sexually explicit (15- and 18-rated) videos (which usually have representative boxes) away from child's-eye level. If they already do, tell them you appreciate it.

5. Write, if necessary, to the British Board of Film Classification if you have complaints about specific titles.
6. Pray a great deal.

Having removed one evil does not entitle us to dismantle the defences.

Notes

I have not documented all my sources. I have selected those which may be helpful to parents wishing to read further, and in some cases notes have been added for clarification.

Chapter 1

1. David Porter, *The Media: a Christian Point of View* (Scripture Union, 1974).
2. See chapter 10.
3. Figures taken from Michael Leroy, 'Liverpool 8 update', *Third Way,* July–August 1984, p.15.
4. Quotations from a transcript supplied by the Press Office, No. 10 Downing Street.
5. 1983 references are contained in the *Annual Report 1984* (NSPCC, 1984).
6. *The Bible and Children's Rights* (Nationwide Festival of Light, n.d.).
7. 'CARE Trust: Mandate for the 1980s', *CARE Trust News,* April–May 1985, p.32.
8. Newsletter of CARE Campaigns, 8 November 1985.
9. See e.g. 'Chamber of Horrors', *Family,* February 1985, p.25.
10. A recent study, for example, is Barrie Gunter, *Dimensions of Television Violence* (Gower, 1985). Gunter's re-

search was sponsored by the IBA. The book contains extensive statistics and analyses.

Chapter 2

1. *Social Trends 1985* (Central Statistical Office, 1985), p.150.
2. *Ibid.,* p.150.
3. A point made in his BBC radio programme, *Soundings,* in a 1985 feature on soap opera.
4. *Ibid.,* p.99.
5. Discussed in e.g. James Britton, *Language and Learning* (Pelican, 1972), pp.33ff.
6. Patricia Marks Greenfield, *Mind and Media: the Effects of Television, Computers and Video Games* (Fontana, 1984), pp.8ff.
7. J. R. Dominick and B. S. Greenberg, 'Attitudes towards Violence: the Interaction of Television, Family Attitudes and Social Class' in G. A. Comstock and E. A. Rubenstein (eds.), *Television and Social Behaviour, vol. III: Television and Adolescent Aggressiveness* (US Government Printing Office, Washington DC, USA, 1972).
8. 'Lord Lane blames TV violence for nastier crime' *Daily Telegraph,* 10 July 1985.
9. Leslie Halliwell, *Halliwell's Film Guide* (Granada, updated occasionally). Halliwell's *Filmgoer's Companion* and his reference books on television and video films, from the same publisher, are also well worth exploring.
10. *Social Trends,* p.150.
11. On the *Black and White Media Show.*
12. CARE Trust's leaflet is available direct from the Trust; Mary Whitehouse's book is *Mightier Than the Sword* (Kingsway Publications, 1985).
13. Viewers who are particularly interested in the issues raised in this chapter may wish to read further about broadcasting standards and the authorities' own perception of

their responsibilities and application of Codes of Practice. Useful resources are *Airwaves,* the quarterly journal of the IBA, and the BBC's *The Listener.*

Chapter 3

1. The figures for 1947 and details of surveys are taken from A. Morgan Derham, *What's Wrong with the Cinema?* (CSSM, 1947).
2. *Social Trends,* p.150.
3. *Britain 1984: an Official Handbook* (HMSO, 1984), p.351.
4. John Ellis, *Visible Fictions: Cinema, Television, Video* (Routledge and Kegan Paul, 1982).
5. I have discussed these points at greater length in my chapter on television in Tim Dean and David Porter (eds.), *Arts in Question* (Marshall Pickering, 1986).
6. The difference between how the phosphor screen of television and the reflective screen of cinema are used aesthetically is a factor that has not yet been adequately discussed.
7. Spielberg made this comment in an Easter 1985 television spectacular in which details of the special effects in the making of the film were revealed.
8. I have discussed these categories with a member of the British Board of Film Censors, and it is quite apparent that there is a high degree of sensitivity to children's needs.

Chapter 4

1. Tracy Kidder, *The Soul of a New Machine* (Penguin, 1982).
2. Patricia Marks Greenfield, *op.cit.*
3. There is little point in giving documentation on piracy, as virtually every hobbyist computer magazine discusses the issue frequently and the correspondence columns are often used to continue the debate. The magazines themselves have been generally opposed to piracy.

4. Hugo Cornwall, *The Hacker's Handbook* (Century Communications, 1985), p.110.

5. *Ibid.,* p.x.

6. 'Teaching hackers ethics', *Newsweek,* 14 January 1985.

7. 'Computer youngsters arrested over War Games plot', *Daily Mail,* 18 July 1985. During the second half of 1985 there were a number of police actions and lawsuits involving hackers.

Chapter 5

1. 'Wargame group in cave probe', *Chislehurst Times,* 18 July 1985.

2. John Weldon and James Bjornstad, *Playing with Fire* (Moody Press, Chicago, USA, 1984), p.18.

3. This story has often been exaggerated in the telling, as is pointed out in e.g. J. Eric Holmes, *Fantasy Role-Playing Games* (Arms and Armour Press, 1981), p.203.

4. Kim Task, 'Off the Wall', *Adventure Gaming,* February 1982, p.4.

5. John Weldon and James Bjornstadt, *op. cit.,* pp.82ff.

6. The point about Elric has been made often in Christian publications.

7. For example in the episode of Saul and the Witch of Endor, 1 Samuel chapter 28, where Saul is rebuked.

8. For Lovecraft see chapter 6.

9. Parents wishing to have a thorough description of the game from people who play it regularly will find helpful John Butterfield, Philip Parker and David Honigman, *What Is Dungeons and Dragons?* (Penguin, 1982). Ian Livingstone's *Dicing with Dragons: an Introduction to Role-Playing Games* (Routledge and Kegan Paul, 1982) and Bruce Galloway, *Fantasy Wargaming* (Patrick Stephens, Cambridge, 1981) are helpful on FRP in general. A simple introduction is Steve Jackson, *Fighting Fantasy* (Puffin, 1984). An excellent catalogue of games from a number of publishers is *The Good*

Games Guide 1: a Comprehensive Guide to Fantasy Gaming (Games Workshop, 1985). I do not necessarily endorse its recommendations.

10. J. Eric Holmes, *op.cit.*, p.99.

11. Quoted in *Forward* (Christian Research Institute, USA), Vol 4. No. 2.

12. Lewis Pulsipher, 'Dungeon Mastering Styles' in *The Best of White Dwarf Articles, volume II* (Games Workshop Ltd, 1983), p.13. The Dungeons and Dragons *Battlesystem* (1985) takes the game back to its origins, with components that look very like a conventional board wargame's.

13. *New West,* 25 August 1980, p.39.

14. Sandy Petersen, *Call of Cthulhu* (Games Workshop Ltd, 2nd ed. 1983), p.49.

15. Herbie Brennan, *Ascent to Hell* (Yaquinto Publications, Texas, USA, 1982), p.14.

16. Gary Gygax and Dave Arnesen, revised by Frank Mentzer, *Dungeons and Dragons: Dungeon Masters Rulebook* (TSR Hobbies Inc., USA, 1983), p.39.

17. *Advanced D&D: Dungeon Master's Guide,* p.220.

Chapter 6

1. H. P. Lovecraft, *The H. P. Lovecraft Omnibus 2: Dagon and Other Macabre Tales* (Panther, 1985).

2. The descriptions given are taken from the second edition rulebook. See chapter 5 note 14 above.

Chapter 7

1. Joe Dever and Gary Chalk, *The Chasm of Doom* (Arrow, 1985), para. 73.

2. Steve Jackson, *House of Hell* (Puffin, 1984), para. 236.

3. The Edgar Wallace and Dennis Wheatley titles are now out of print. Kit Williams's books are published by Jonathan

Cape. Metagaming, at the time of writing, has ceased trading. All the Metagaming treasures have been discovered, and the Pimania sundial was discovered just as this book went to press.

4. Rose Estes, *Dragon of Doom* (TSR Inc., USA, 1983).

5. Steve Jackson, *Fighting Fantasy* (Puffin, 1984).

6. Steve Jackson and Ian Livingstone, *The Warlock of Firetop Mountain* (Puffin, 1982).

7. Margaret Weis, *Tower of Midnight Dreams* (TSR Inc., 1985).

8. Roald Dahl, 'Tales we mustn't tell our children', *Daily Mail,* 4 May 1984.

9. Stephen King, *Night Shift* (New English Library, 1978), p.17.

10. *Scream! Holiday Special* (IPC Magazines Ltd., May 1985).

11. It is another name for a vampire.

Chapter 8

1. J. R. R. Tolkien, *The Lord of the Rings* (3 vols, George Allen and Unwin, 1954).

2. J. R. R. Tolkien, *The Hobbit* (George Allen and Unwin, 3rd edition 1966).

3. C. S. Lewis, *The Lion, the Witch and the Wardrobe* (Penguin, 1959).

4. John Houghton, *Hagbane's Doom* (Kingsway Publications, 1984), and *Gublak's Greed* (Kingsway Publications, 1985).

5. John White, *The Tower of Geburah* (Kingsway Publications, 1984).

6. All published in the UK by Lion Publishing, 1985.

7. Also published by Lion, 1984.

8. Fay Sampson: *Pangbur Ban the White Cat* (Lion Publishing, 1983); *Finnglas of the Horses* (Lion Publishing, 1984).

9. *The Wind in the Willows* is by Kenneth Grahame; *Watership Down* is by Richard Adams.

10. Paul Kocher, *Master of Middle-Earth: the Achievement of J. R. R. Tolkien* (Penguin, 1972).

11, 12. Both are published by Iron Crown Enterprises in the USA and are distributed in this country by Games Workshop Ltd, 27–29 Sunbeam Road, London NW10 6JP.

13. Published by Avalon Hill, whose UK address is Avalon Hill Games, 650 High Street, London N12.

14. Published by Melbourne House, 131 Trafalgar Road, London SE10. A copy of the book is included in the price.

15. Published by Beyond Software, Lector Court, 151 Farringdon Road, London EC1R 3AD.

16. Published by Level 9 Computing, 229 Hughenden Road, High Wycombe, Buckinghamshire.

17. Published by Sound and Vision Unit, Scripture Union, 130 City Road, London EC1V 2NJ.

18. Published by Micro Power Ltd, Sheepscar House, Sheepscar Street South, Leeds LS7 1AD.

19. I am grateful to the Editor of the *Gazette* for permission to quote this comment. The quotation from Beyond Software is from correspondence between *Beyond* and the author.

20. For example, Martin Barker (ed.), *The Video Nasties: Freedom and Censorship in the Media* (Pluto Press, 1984); and Martin Barker, *A Haunt of Fears: the Strange History of the British Horror Comics Campaign* (Pluto Press, 1984).

21. See Barker, *op.cit.*, and Fredric Wertham, *Seduction of the Innocent* (Museum Press, 1955).

22. I take this information from an edition of *Redemption Tidings* early in 1985. It describes efforts by the Coalition to get 'required warnings on all D&D game materials'.

Chapter 9

1. Derived from a number of sources, some of which are documented below.

2. For example, a much-quoted survey is 'Child Sex Abuse'

by Tony Baker. This was a confidential survey among readers of *19* magazine.

3. Quoted in Yvonne Roberts, 'When is a child in safe hands?', *Daily Post,* 18 May 1984.

4. Figures are becoming available from the NSPCC based on these registers. E.g. in *Characteristics of the Sexually Abused Child and Its Family* (a document prepared by its Research Officer in July 1984), and Information Sheet No.2, *Incidence of Child Sexual Abuse* (31 October 1984).

5. Fiona Goble, 'Child Sexual Abuse: the Unspeakable Crime', *The Children's Friend* (magazine of the NSPCC), May 1985.

6. Information Sheet No.2, *op.cit.*

7. I am grateful to a counsellor from the Tavistock Institute for an account of these services.

8. This section is largely based on personal conversation with Mr Oxley.

9. 'Child sex crusader: angry head who joined PIE to spy', *Daily Mail,* 7 November 1984.

10. Gita Sereny, *The Invisible Children* (André Deutsch, 1984).

11. Gita Sereny, 'Lost innocence of the rejected children', *The Times,* 21 September 1984.

12. Rodney Clapp, 'The Children of the Cults', *Christianity Today* (USA), 4 March 1983.

13. Deo Gloria Trust also sponsors Christian Response to the Occult, which publishes a number of leaflets which are relevant to subjects in this book.

14. As listed in the *Evening Standard*'s entertainment pages. I have not personally investigated these films, but saw Jean-Luc Godard's *Numero Deux.*

15. Ian Cooper, *Abortion? A Briefing Note* (Order of Christian Unity, 1981) is a useful summary of the position in ten pages.

16. Relevant statistics can be obtained from many sources, e.g. *Social Trends.* Summaries frequently appear in the

Press; e.g. 'Facts and Families', *Care News,* February–March 1984.

17. *Characteristics of the Sexually Abused Child and Its Family, op. cit.*

18. Private correspondence with the author. A recent study of this subject is Elsa Ferri, *Stepchildren: a National Study* (NFER-Nelson, 1984).

19. 'Molester given a job caring for children', *Daily Mail,* 7 December 1984.

20. This is, for example, the policy of the Hampshire police (information provided by Winchester police public relations department).

21. Michele Elliott, *Preventing Child Sexual Assault: a Practical Guide to Talking with Children* (Bedford Square Press, 2nd edition 1985; published in association with Child Assault Prevention Programme). I am grateful to the publishers for letting me see advance proofs of the second edition.

Chapter 10

1. This story ran in local and national newspapers during July–August 1985: e.g. 'A dying addict of 14', *Daily Mail,* 31 July 1985; 'Jason's dad on heroin', *Liverpool Echo,* 7 August 1985.

2. 'Terrible toll of the drug kids', *Liverpool Echo,* 5 August 1985.

3. 'Schools drug watch by undercover police', *Evening Standard,* 10 July 1985.

4. 'Junkie baby "ill-treated in the womb"' *Daily Mail,* 24 July 1985.

5. 'Heroin addicts doomed to die', *Daily Mail,* 21 June 1985.

6. 'In this city you don't go looking for drugs . . . they come looking for you', *Daily Express,* 20 May 1985.

7. Information on these and a number of other drugs can be found in *Drug Misuse: a Basic Briefing* (Department of Health and Social Security, 1985). This is a short booklet.

The Department issues a number of related leaflets. Further information is obtainable from your local Health Education Unit, whose telephone number is in local telephone directories.

8. 'Cocaine warfare', *Daily Mail,* 23 January 1985.

9. Stacy Keach, 'The diabolical hell of cocaine', *Daily Express,* 17 December 1984.

10. E.g. 'Some of the most famous faces you see on TV are snorting cocaine', *Daily Mail,* 25 March 1985.

11. Examples and case-histories are given in *What Parents Can Do about Drugs,* obtainable from the Department of Health and Social Security.

12. 'The rich victims of the drug craze', *Daily Mail,* 20 March 1985.

13. 'On patrol: Warden to beat glue peril', *Daily Express,* 2 August 1985. Parents needing guidance on glue-sniffing will find useful the Health Education Council's leaflet, *What to Do about Glue-Sniffing.*

Appendix

1. *Report of a Parliamentary Group Video Enquiry: Video Violence and Children. Part I: Children's Viewing Patterns in England & Wales* (Oasis Projects, 1983); *Part II: Children's Viewing Patterns and Parental Attitudes in England & Wales* (Oasis Projects, 1984); *Part III: Video Violence and Children* (Hodder and Stoughton, 1985).

2. *Ibid.,* Part I, p.2.

3. *Ibid.,* Part II, sec. 2.34.

4. Martin Barker (ed.), *The Video Nasties: Freedom and Censorship in the Media* (Pluto Press, 1984). I have summarized a number of contributors' arguments in the following paragraphs.

5. *Ibid.,* p.47.

6. *Ibid.,* p.46.

7. Point made in personal conversation with the author.

8. Report, *op.cit.*, Part II, sec. A.27.

9. *Ibid.*, sect. A.22.

10. Polly Toynbee, 'Why nasty is as nasty does', *The Guardian*, 13 March 1984.

For the Children's Sake
*Educational Foundations
for Home and School*

by Susan Schaeffer Macaulay

We all want the best for our children, both at home and at school. Susan Schaeffer Macaulay shows from Christian educational principles and from her own experience as a mother what part we can play in the awakening of our children's minds.

Susan shows how education should begin with a true understanding of each child as a unique individual made in the image of God. Rejecting any theory that cramps and discourages that precious personality, she proposes an approach that warms and stimulates children to fulfil their true potential. To be part of our children's education then becomes a life-enriching experience, and discipline takes its proper place in a context of love and encouragement.

Parents and teachers alike will value this positive approach at a time when much modern educational theory is undergoing serious review.

'Education is an adventure...it's about people, children, life, reality!'

Susan Schaeffer Macaulay is the daughter of Francis and Edith Schaeffer. She and her husband Ranald brought up their four children at the L'Abri Community in England, before moving on to Switzerland where Ranald is now International Director of L'Abri.

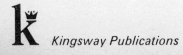

Kingsway Publications

Stats – how many kids r
at risk from
abuse 2day –